Welcome to Alaska!

We hope you'll find this book a kind of chatty traveling companion for your journey, opening doors and drawing character sketches of the places and things you'll meet. With a combination of facts and history and comments— and an occasional tall tale—we hope both to satisfy your curiosity and to whet your appetite.

Southwest &
the Aleutians

Southcentral

Arctic & Western

© 1985 Harald Sund

© 1985 Mark Kelley / Alaska Photo

Interior

Southeast

© 1985 Art Wolfe / Alaska Photo

Contents

Alaska Lingo

*W*e offer here a guide to some of the words and phrases, some ancient and some of recent vintage, known only to the vocabulary of Alaska.

"CAMAI!" (Cha-my) A warm greeting: "Hello!" . . . "Nice to see you!" . . . "Good luck!" in Yupik, one of the two major Eskimo languages spoken in Alaska. (The word is loosely comparable in meaning to the Hawaiian "Aloha!")

OUTSIDE Anywhere outside Alaska (except Canada, where conditions so closely resemble those of Alaska), but generally refers to the contiguous 48 states.

SOUTH 48
Term adopted after Alaska became a state in 1959, to distinguish the contiguous 48 states from the rest of the Outside. (Alaska is one-fifth the size of the combined South 48.)

ALCAN Original name for the highway through ALaska and CANada now known as the Alaska Highway. During the 50's, used cars which had been shipped (rather than driven over the gravel Alcan) were advertised under the proud label "NO ALCAN."

PANHANDLE The Southeast region of Alaska, which dangles below the mainland of the state like a handle from a frying pan (the description would also fit the Alaska Peninsula, which similarly protrudes from the bottom of the opposite (western) corner.

PARKA A one-piece slipover coat with a hood, associated chiefly with Eskimos but used to some extent by most Alaska Native people. The classic cold weather parka was made of caribou hide, with a ruff of wolf fur, lined with wolverine, around the face opening of the hood. Waterproof parkas used by whaling men were made from seal intestines.

KUSPUK Hooded garment of brightly colored cotton print, made as a cover for traditional parkas, but also worn as a dress or light jacket for warm weather.

ESKIMO ICE CREAM Animal fat (often caribou or seal) whipped to a creamy texture and mixed with chopped meat (northern region) or berries (west and southwest regions).

UMIAK Boat used by Eskimos and Aleuts, made of hide stretched over a light frame of driftwood. Usually about 40 ft.

long, umiaks could be carried by two men and carry two tons of freight on water.

MUKTUK An Eskimo delicacy consisting of the skin and attached layer of whale blubber (fat). Sometimes eaten dried or cooked, but usually raw.

POTLATCH Old Indian and Eskimo custom: a gathering to celebrate an occasion or event, at which the host demonstrates his affluence by distributing gifts to the guests—who then attempt to top this generosity with even more lavish gifts at a potlatch of their own. (The modern version is usually a combination party and feast without the emphasis on gifts.)

CACHE A small structure resembling a cabin, e l e v a t e d above ground on long legs of log, used by bush people to protect food and belongings from foraging animals.

TUNDRA Northern areas covered by low-lying vegetation, without trees, underlain by permanently frozen soil ("permafrost").

MUSKEG Swamp or bog, often used incorrectly as a synonym for tundra (although much of the tundra region does indeed consist of muskeg).

TERMINATION DUST First annual snow to appear on mountain tops. During the building boom following World War II, seasonal construction workers saw the first sign of snow as a signal that their jobs would soon be terminated for the year.

THE BUSH Those very sizable parts of Alaska remote from the highway system; rural communities and surroundings; the "boondocks," or back country.

BUSH PILOTS Pilots of the light planes, often equipped with floats or skis, which provide transportation to, from and between Alaska's bush communities and other isolated destinations. They also deliver and pick up hunters, fishermen and other urban people "escaping" on outings to the hinterlands. Bush pilots were key to the settlement of Alaska long before the modern highway system developed.

SQUAW CANDY Strips of fish meat (usually salmon) air dried, heated and smoked over an open fire. Whole or half fish thus prepared are often used as dog food, but strips of good fish meat are considered a true delicacy by Natives and non-Natives alike.

BREAKUP The spring melting season—virtually a season unto itself—which heralds the blossoming of horrendous potholes in city streets, and tough going for foot traffic in the bush. Despite such adverse effects it is a time of jubilation and rejuvenation for Alaskans bleary-eyed from long, long, long winter nights.

ICE FOG

Tiny ice particles formed from vapor when the air becomes too cold to retain moisture. The effect is that of a thick winter fog.

PERMA-FROST

Soil, throughout the Alaska Arctic and in much of the Interior Region, which is permanently frozen.

ARCTIC CIRCLE

The parallel of latitude at North 66 degrees, 33 minutes. While it technically marks the world's "Frigid Zone," the Arctic Circle crosses Alaska's Interior Region far below the Brooks Mountain Range where the Alaskan Arctic Region begins.

PERMANENT FUND

A state "savings account," created by a constitutional amendment, requiring at least 25% of Alaska's royalties from oil and other minerals to be set aside, with only the income from interest earnings available for spending.

How to tell a Cheechako from a Sourdough

Alaskan version of "tenderfoot," or newcomer (as distinguished from a visitor).

Cheechako

First of all, why bother? They both plan to move to Palm Springs as soon as they strike gold or oil.

But here are some tell-tale signs:

Mosquitoes always move *from* the Sourdough *to* the Cheechako. The reason is known only to Sourdoughs, but by the time you're old enough to be a Sourdough you're too smart to go around explaining mosquito behavior to Cheechakos. (Hence the expression: "Twice bitten, once shy.")

The Cheechako always packs enough luggage to provide clothing for any emergency. The Sourdough doesn't worry about luggage because his clothing *is* an emergency.

The Cheechako always carries a camera, hoping to photograph a charging grizzly bear. The Sourdough always carries a bear rug, hoping to charge a Cheechako for taking a picture.

The Cheechako carries lots of maps so he won't get lost in the dense wilderness. The Sourdough *wants* to get lost in the wilderness, but keeps running into dense Cheechakos with maps.

SUNDOG

Large bright spots appearing on opposite sides of the sun in wintertime, caused by refraction of sunlight through ice crystals suspended in the air. The condition can also create an apparent ring of light around the sun.

SITKA SLIPPERS

Knee-high rubber boots worn by fishermen, also serving as all-purpose footwear for residents of some particularly damp communities.

QIVIUT

Soft underhair of musk-oxen, considered one of the world's rarest fibers, spun into yarn for knitting highly prized sweaters, gloves and scarves. Alaska's native musk-oxen were hunted to extinction by mid 19th century, but transplants from Greenland in 1930 have multiplied to a population of about 1,500 distributed among several Alaska sites and protected by law.

NO-SEE-UM

Tiny winged insects (a form of gnat), nearly invisible, whose bite produces an itchy welt only slightly less irritating than a crocodile attack. They are found near water (actually, they find you) and seem most numerous in late summer.

CABIN FEVER

A condition—similar to what a stick of dynamite must feel just before it explodes —which afflicts people confined indoors during long, dark winter nights. It can make a single, solitary person feel surrounded by nincompoops, and even a frying pan seems to acquire an irritating personality.

"KUYANAK!"

(Koy-ah-nuk) "Thank you!" spoken in Inupiaq, the other major Alaska Eskimo language. (So distinctly different are Yupik and Inupiaq that non English-speaking Eskimos may need an interpreter in order to converse.)

An oldtimer, from the days when prospectors and other wanderers carried a lump of fermented starter dough for making bread.

Sourdough

Cheechakos change socks every day and tend to lose their boots in the soggy muskeg. Sourdoughs are born with socks and shoes which molt every five or six years, to be replaced by a new growth known as "boondockers." Cheechakos exaggerate facts. Sourdoughs exaggerate wild rumors.

Southeast Alaska

Yakutat · Skagway · Haines · Juneau · Glacier Bay · Petersburg · Wrangell · Sitka · Ketchikan

*S*outheast Alaska—"The Panhandle"—is an archipelago of more than 1,000 islands, clustered along a narrow 400-mile strip of mountainous coastline. Among its forests, waters and mountain passes have transpired some of the most vivid dramas in Alaskan history.

Ketchikan

Ketchikan, first port of call in Alaska for north-bound ships, stretches like a ribbon along a narrow shelf of shoreline squeezed between Tongass Narrows and the slope of Deer Mountain. Much of its business district extends over the water on pilings, and few buildings in the town seem more than a stone's throw from splash.

Ketchikan is the epitome of a waterfront town. It seems to reverberate with the whistling, creaking and churning of boats and tugs and barges and ships, large and small, ever on the move along its shores.

Its site on the mouth of Ketchikan Creek, once used for Indian fishing camps, saw a short-lived cannery and a failed trading post during the late 1880's. Nearby discoveries of gold and copper then gave rise to a booming mining center whose population reached 800 at the turn of the century.

A new cannery began operating, a lumber mill arose to supply the cannery, and when the mining boom fold-

Ketchikan 1905

9

ed in 1907 Ketchikan's fishery was strong enough to sustain the community. Commercial fishing peaked during the 1930's and began declining in the '40's, but it still accounts, along with tourism and sports fishing, for much of the hustle and bustle along the waterfront. A pulp mill 7 miles north of town became the town's economic mainstay in 1954, but has encountered difficulties in recent years.

Echoes of pioneer days still haunt Creek Street, built on pilings along Ketchikan Creek, where for half a century two dozen sporting houses brought romance—albeit for a price —into the lives of lonely miners, loggers and fishermen.

A much earlier era is evoked at the Totem Heritage Cultural Center, enclosing Alaska's largest collection of original totem poles. Totem Bight park, 10 miles from town, displays 13 totems near a re-created Tlingit Indian Community House.

Petersburg

Petersburg, on Mitkof Island, is that rare Southeast Alaska community with no historical ties to the Russian occupation or to gold or Indian settlement. "Little Norway," it is called, for the town was cleared from a virgin shore by Scandinavian fishermen who were mostly Norwegian.

They came with the first cannery in 1900, and their Scandinavian character molded the place. Snugly framed by forests to the east and sprawling Kupreanof Island

Ketchikan faces on the water not just horizontally, but vertically as well: average annual precipitation is 154 inches. Residents good naturedly measure their "liquid sunshine" in terms of feet, and the record exceeds 16.

Wrangell

In the glow of evening, as a falling sun silhouettes the cluster of neighboring islands which shelter Wrangell from the sea, there is something about the town which suggests small-town America. But its heritage runs deep and rich.

First there were Tlingit Indians, and some of Alaska's most ancient totem poles now stand on Chief Shakes Island near the center of town.

Russian fur traders came to build Fort Dionysius in 1834. The Russians then leased all of Southeast Alaska to the British Hudsons' Bay Co., which changed the name to Fort Stikine. Abandoned in 1850, it was reoccupied as Fort Wrangell by the American Army following the Alaska Purchase of 1867.

Gold miners enroute to the Stikine River created a 5-year surge of activity which ended in 1877. But that same year brought construction of the first of many fish canneries which—together with the lumber industry to serve the canneries—have provided the backbone of Wrangell's economy ever since.

across a narrow channel to the west, maritime Petersburg somehow exudes the solid feel of an inland village.

Situated amidst some of Alaska's richest waters, Petersburg, although it serves nearby logging operations, remains devoted primarily to fishing. It has produced one of the world's foremost halibut fleets, and the tiny, tasty Petersburg shrimp is a delicacy of international renown.

Each May the town celebrates Norwegian Independence Day with a lively "Little Norway Festival." Just a short boat or plane trip away is Le Conte Glacier, southernmost tidewater glacier on the continent.

A Tlingit canoe shows the flag at Chief Shakes Island. (Probably early 1900's)

The Anchorage Museum

Sitka
A Profile of Russian Heritage

Every visitor to Sitka should make the short climb to the top of Castle Hill and there, standing next to one of the ancient Russian cannon, gaze out over Sitka Sound toward the ocean horizon.

Here, many times, must have stood Lord Alexander Baranof, the doughty leader who explored and ruled Alaska for the Russian-American Company under a charter from the Czar. It takes but little imagination to see, as he did, the sailing ships rocking at anchor, or the Tlingit Indian canoes passing among the dozens of islets which dot the waters off Sitka.

On this spot Baranof built the log and frame structure, known as Baranof's Castle, which served as his home and as headquarters for far-flung enterprises reaching as far as Hawaii and California. Here, for half a century, lay the heart of Russia's American empire.

The Russians, reaching

southward 600 miles from their base on Kodiak Island, had established their first Southeast Alaska outpost in 1799 near the site of modern Sitka. They were quickly expelled by Tlingit Indian attacks, but Baranof returned in 1804 with enough manpower and cannon to defeat the Tlingits on a battleground now occupied by Sitka National Historical Park. He then built a new town, which would become Sitka, at the present locale.

Baranof moved the headquarters of the Russian-American Company from Kodiak to Sitka in 1806. As the hub of that prosperous fur trading monopoly it became known during the early 1800's as "The Paris of the Pacific," the largest city on the west coast. Its facilities included sawmills, tanneries, shipyards, and a foundry which cast bells for many of the Spanish missions scattered throughout California. In the mansion on the hill (to be destroyed and rebuilt three times over the years) Baranof and his successors hosted lavish entertainments for ship captains come to trade from ports around the world.

St. Michael's Russian Orthodox Cathedral, built in the 1840's (and reconstructed from original blueprints after a 1966 fire) still looms over the town.

But the Russian enterprise was far deteriorated when the United States purchased Alaska in 1867. Sitka became a quiet mining and fishing community, the home of Sheldon Jackson College and the Pioneer's Home, Alaska's seat of government from 1867 to 1900, and location for a variety of federal agency offices.

Construction of a huge pulp mill in 1959 greatly accelerated an economy then based primarily on fishing. Since then tourism—nourished by a wealth of Russian and Tlingit history amid eye-filling seascapes—has grown apace with the coming of state

"Baranof's Castle," 1899. St. Michael's Cathedral at right.

ferry traffic, construction of the bridge connecting Sitka with its jet airport on Japonski Island, and Sitka's growing reputation as a cultural, historical and recreational center.

A haunting walk through the Historical Park, past Tlingit totem poles scattered along the way, leads to the site of the Indian fort destroyed by Baranof after the battle of 1804.

Did You Know?

From lakes near Sitka the enterprising Russians cut blocks of ice which they shipped for sale to the up-and-coming town of San Francisco.

For years ships carried letters between Baranof and King Kamehameha of Hawaii, who invited the Russian to retire to his islands. However they never met.

Juneau

Approaching Alaska's capital city by either sea or air, the eye is captured first by the tall buildings which dominate the skyline—state and federal government offices which generate the bulk of Juneau's economic life.

But standing apart on the mountainside, to the south of the city, is the burned-out hulk of the AJ Mining Company mill—a reminder of earlier days when Juneau pioneers were sluicing the gravel and blasting the tunnels which would make it one of the most productive gold mining areas in the world.

Congress transferred the Territorial

capital from Sitka to Juneau in 1900, but as the move was completed in 1906 Juneau was absorbed in mining and fishing. By the time World War II closed the last mine, the AJ, after half a century of hardrock mining, Juneau had become a labor and supply base for the regional fish canning industry and acquired a position as crossroads for commerce and transportation in the Territory.

Juneau's famous Taku winds can stir the air even more vigorously than a session of the legislature, but the Takus blow only intermittently.

The post-war succession of booms within Alaska ultimately led to statehood and made Juneau's role as state capital a growth industry in itself. Commercial fishing and an expanding tourist industry augment government to provide the city's basic sources of employment.

Juneau's 20,000 plus people live mostly in the Mendenhall Valley 10 miles north of downtown, along the road leading to it, and on Douglas Island, connected to downtown by a bridge across narrow Gastineau Channel.

Winter & Pond Collection/Alaska Historical Library

Juneau 1895

Did You Know?

Each January 60 legislators assemble in Juneau to lubricate the wheels of progress with a state income, 85% derived from oil, averaging about $3 ½ billion annually over the past few years. The urge for mining gold still runs in the veins, however; legislators are often heard to exclaim, with great passion, "Mine, mine, mine!"

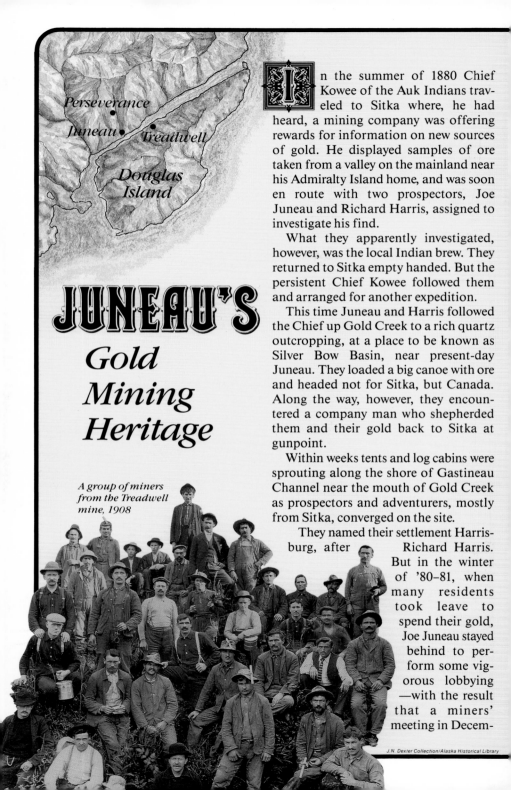

Perseverance

Juneau • Treadwell

Douglas Island

JUNEAU'S
Gold Mining Heritage

A group of miners from the Treadwell mine, 1908

In the summer of 1880 Chief Kowee of the Auk Indians traveled to Sitka where, he had heard, a mining company was offering rewards for information on new sources of gold. He displayed samples of ore taken from a valley on the mainland near his Admiralty Island home, and was soon en route with two prospectors, Joe Juneau and Richard Harris, assigned to investigate his find.

What they apparently investigated, however, was the local Indian brew. They returned to Sitka empty handed. But the persistent Chief Kowee followed them and arranged for another expedition.

This time Juneau and Harris followed the Chief up Gold Creek to a rich quartz outcropping, at a place to be known as Silver Bow Basin, near present-day Juneau. They loaded a big canoe with ore and headed not for Sitka, but Canada. Along the way, however, they encountered a company man who shepherded them and their gold back to Sitka at gunpoint.

Within weeks tents and log cabins were sprouting along the shore of Gastineau Channel near the mouth of Gold Creek as prospectors and adventurers, mostly from Sitka, converged on the site.

They named their settlement Harrisburg, after Richard Harris. But in the winter of '80–81, when many residents took leave to spend their gold, Joe Juneau stayed behind to perform some vigorous lobbying —with the result that a miners' meeting in Decem-

The AJ Mining Company mill started operation in 1917. Today, its ruins remain on the hillside south of Juneau.

ber voted to change the name to Juneau, the one that stuck.

There is no record of what rewards Chief Kowee may have garnered from his travails, but his efforts paid handsome dividends to posterity. For he had pointed to a massive ore deposit which, it would eventually be learned, extended 1,500 ft. below the surface at Douglas Island and rose 2,000 ft. above sea level in the mountains behind Juneau.

Today Mt. Juneau and Mt. Roberts are honeycombed with mile after mile of abandoned tunnels and shafts which— along with the prolific Treadwell mine on Douglas Island—yielded upwards of $150 million in gold during times when the price was but $35 an ounce.

Juneau now runs on oil. But its narrow, winding streets, and its wooden stairs climbing the mountain sides, remain as cherished legacies of days that glistened gold.

Inside the Treadwell operation

The Perseverance quartz mills in Silver Bow Basin, 1907

Mendenhall Glacier

The glacier close to the old A.J. Power House in 1912

I n the coastal mountains behind Juneau the snow falls at an annual rate of 100 feet or more, over the years compressing itself from its own weight into a 1,500-square-mile pack of ice known as the Juneau Ice Field. Its enormous pressures squeeze rivers of ice—glaciers—down mountain valleys and slopes. One of the most accessible, Mendenhall Glacier, terminates just 14 miles from downtown Juneau in a wall of ice 200 feet high and 1½ miles wide. Tour buses deliver visitors to a U.S. Forest Service observation and information center not far from the glacier face.

I n 1897 and '98 thousands of gold rush stampeders boarded ships bound for boomtown Skagway, at the tip of Lynn Canal, a thin finger of water extending northward above Juneau for 75 spectacular miles. Since those days the sights and sounds of that passage have scarcely changed. The gold seekers must have seen the great bald eagles perched in trees along the narrow channel, or swooping low to the blue water. And despite their obsession with gold, they must have been awed by the humpback whales arching their gigantic flukes above the surface as they dived. Today, near Skagway, lonely Eldred Rock Lighthouse stands forlorn on a tiny rock, looking very much as though it ought to be haunted by a spectral keeper clad in a billowing black oilskin coat.

The Lynn Canal area is home to the largest population of Bald Eagles in the world.

Lynn Canal

The Eagles of Haines

Naturalists and photographers come to Haines from all over the world to witness one of the most unusual and impressive sights in nature's kingdom. At a place known as Eagle Council Grounds, 20 miles from town along the Haines Highway, upwards of 3,000 American Bald Eagles gather along the Chilkat River. As many as 80 have been seen perched in a single tree, and more than a hundred may be captured within the frame of a single photograph.

A stable population of 15,000 eagles is estimated to inhabit the Southeast Alaska area, and they are seen year round at Haines. What brings so many together in such a small area at Eagle Council Grounds is a minor natural phenomenon: during the winter months, ground water seepage prevents a short stretch of the Chilkat River from freezing over—and so the eagles congregate from September through January in order to pluck late running salmon from the river.

The Alaskan bald eagles frequently attain a wingspan of seven feet, and with their white heads and glinting eyes they present an awe-inspiring sight as they perch in trees or stalk the river banks by the thousands.

I n sharp contrast to its wilderness backdrop, Haines is dominated by a crisp rectangle of

Haines and the Chilkats

neat white buildings—old Fort William H. Seward, established in 1903 to police northern gold camps. The original Haines, adjoining the fort, had begun as a trading post and Presbyterian mission in 1879. Until then the Chilkat Indians, among the most powerful of the Tlingit tribes, had controlled that strategic spot where waterborne commerce of Southeast Alaska connected to ancient trading trails through the mountains into the vast interior. The modern Haines Highway follows much of the route of those Indian pathways. Decommissioned in 1944, the fort was acquired by private owners, renamed Port Chilkoot, and later merged with the original settlement to form the city of Haines. Chilkat history and tradition are vividly portrayed by the world-famous Chilkat Dancers (below) who perform on the original parade ground site of Fort Seward during the summer season.

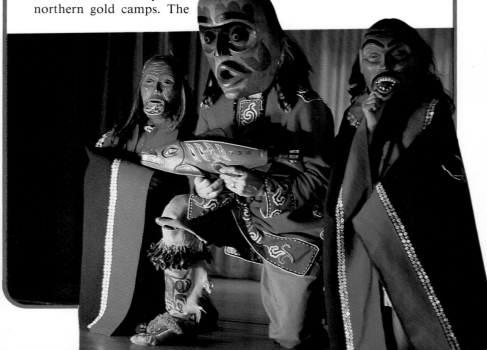

Glacier Bay

Muir Glacier visited by tourists in the early 1900's

Alaska Historical Library

© 1985 Tom Bean / Alaska Photo

How Glaciers Form

Individual glaciers advance or retreat, according to whether their downhill movement is less or greater than the loss from melting and/or calving of icebergs. Although such movement is normally measured in inches or feet per year, Muir Glacier receded an amazing 5 miles in just 7 years.

F or sheer, extravagant, eye-boggling displays of nature in the raw, few north country locales can match the glaciers, waters, rain forests and wildlife of Glacier Bay. Two centuries ago Glacier Bay—just west of Lynn Canal—was a great basin of solid ice left over from the ice age. A warming climate, aided by earthquakes, forced the ice to recede as ocean water moved in to fill the void, creating numerous inlets and fjords along a bay which today is over 60 miles long.

"Thunder Bay" it was called by the Indians, from the booming sounds which roll across the water as colossal slabs of ice—as much as 200 feet long—break from the face of towering glaciers and smash into the sea to become icebergs. Giant cruise ships appear as toy boats against immensities of ice: the face of Muir Glacier is almost two miles wide and rises 265 feet above the water. Muir is but one of 16 major tidewater glaciers (among numerous smaller ones) within the 4,400-square-mile area of Glacier Bay National Park and Preserve.

Wildlife abounds in the waters and skies of Glacier Bay, and in the lush rain forests along the shores near the mouth.

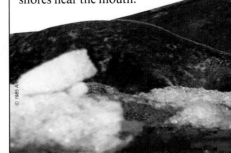

© 1985 An

Looking
for Sea Life

Whales, seals and porpoises are often spotted from cruise boats, as are bears on the beaches and mountain goats on the slopes. More than 200 species of birds also inhabit Glacier Bay.

Killer (Orca) Whale

Beluga Whale

Bowhead Whale

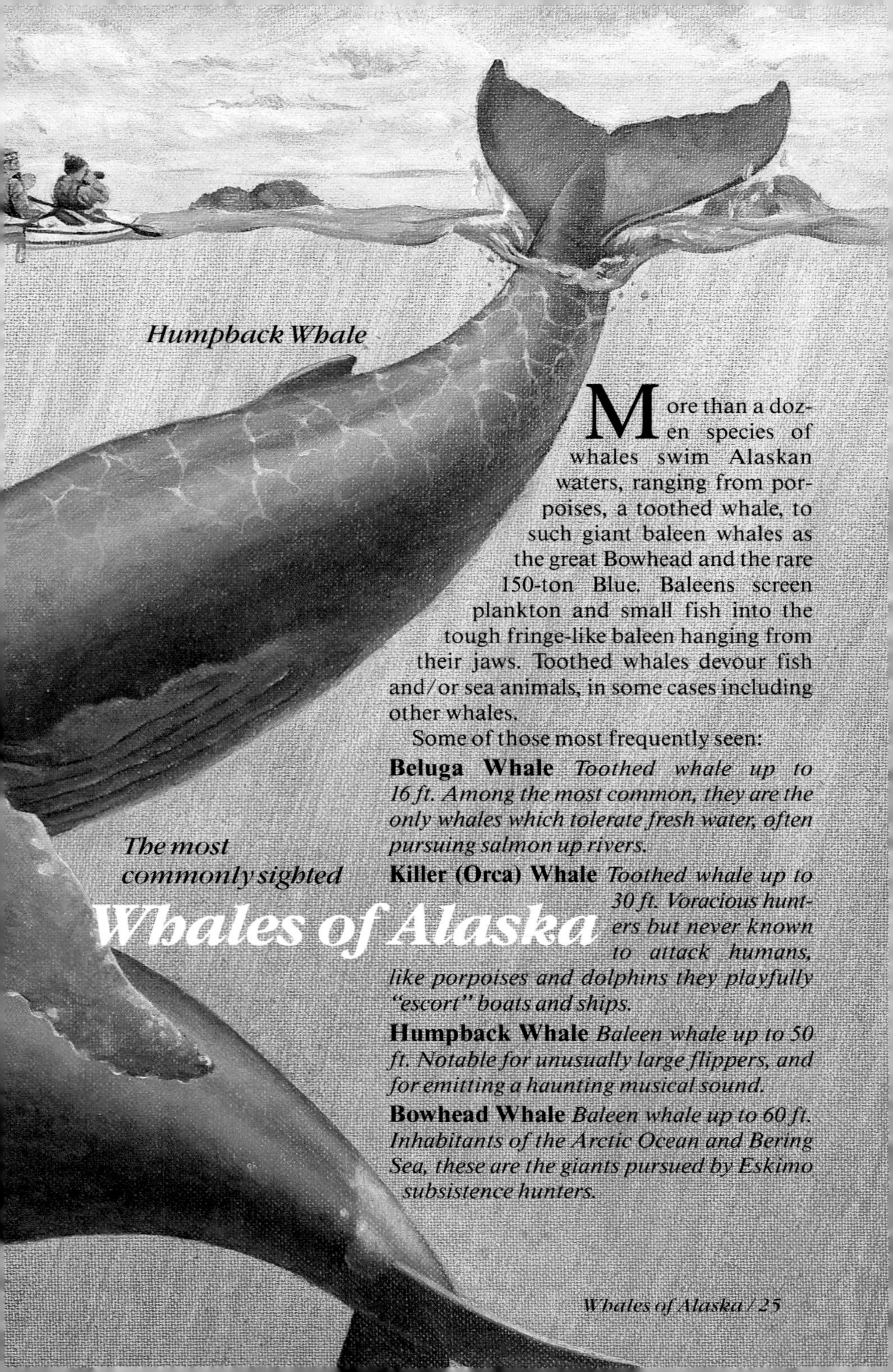

Humpback Whale

M ore than a dozen species of whales swim Alaskan waters, ranging from porpoises, a toothed whale, to such giant baleen whales as the great Bowhead and the rare 150-ton Blue. Baleens screen plankton and small fish into the tough fringe-like baleen hanging from their jaws. Toothed whales devour fish and/or sea animals, in some cases including other whales.

Some of those most frequently seen:

Beluga Whale *Toothed whale up to 16 ft. Among the most common, they are the only whales which tolerate fresh water, often pursuing salmon up rivers.*

The most commonly sighted

Whales of Alaska

Killer (Orca) Whale *Toothed whale up to 30 ft. Voracious hunters but never known to attack humans, like porpoises and dolphins they playfully "escort" boats and ships.*

Humpback Whale *Baleen whale up to 50 ft. Notable for unusually large flippers, and for emitting a haunting musical sound.*

Bowhead Whale *Baleen whale up to 60 ft. Inhabitants of the Arctic Ocean and Bering Sea, these are the giants pursued by Eskimo subsistence hunters.*

© 1985 Harald Sund

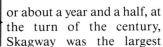

GOLDSMITH

For about a year and a half, at the turn of the century, Skagway was the largest town in Alaska and one of the busiest places in the world. For that brief time it served as gateway to White Pass and a stopover for gold-seekers en route to Dyea trading post at the foot of Chilkoot Pass—the primary routes for thousands of frantic men and women stampeding toward the gold fields of the Klondike.

The stampede lasted less than two years, but Skagway remains a gold rush town still, thanks to the spirit

Skagw

and enthusiasm of its people. They love their history *Wher* and preserve its character and rich flavor—together with its board sidewalks, pebbled streets, false-front stores, and many original gold rush buildings and artifacts.

The atmosphere of Skagway seems to waft from the cover of an old calendar. Though it may suggest a movie set or a Jack London novel, it is a legacy of very real people: 20,000 or more strangers thrown together on a wilderness beach, motivated mostly by hunger or greed, without govern-

This aerial photo of Lynn Canal clearly shows Skagway, gateway to White Pass Trail (far right) and the former site of Dyea, gateway to the Chilkoot Pass Trail (far left).

the Spirit of '98 Lives

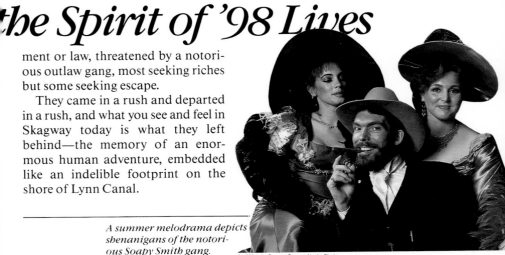

ment or law, threatened by a notorious outlaw gang, most seeking riches but some seeking escape.

They came in a rush and departed in a rush, and what you see and feel in Skagway today is what they left behind—the memory of an enormous human adventure, embedded like an indelible footprint on the shore of Lynn Canal.

A summer melodrama depicts shenanigans of the notorious Soapy Smith gang.

 Captain William Moore was biding his time at his homestead on the mouth of the Skagway River near the tip of Lynn Canal. An old hand in the north country, Moore had predicted that the Yukon River Valley would someday spawn a major gold rush. And so, in 1888, he staked his homestead on tidewater at the foot of White Pass, which he had discovered, and which he deemed superior to Chilkoot Pass, beyond Dyea trading post 5 miles to the north, as a gateway to the Yukon. For 9 years he had waited to make a fortune from the hordes who would anchored off Moore's homestead. They swarmed ashore, seized his land, and hired a surveyor to lay out a new town which would be called Skagway. When the centerline of a street was

Chaos on a Wilderness

one day need his land as a staging area for the gold rush he anticipated.

Unknown to Capt. Moore, miners from the new Yukon River boom town of Dawson City had just disembarked from ships at San Francisco and Seattle, laden with 3 tons of gold dust and nuggets which electrified the nation. Ten days later, July 27, 1897, a shipload of gold stampeders—the first of thousands to come—

Skagway is Born

found to run through Moore's cabin, they evicted him.

As floods of gold seekers followed

"Ma" Pullen sold room and meals to the stampeders and carted their freight over White Pass.

those first arrivals, Skagway erupted into a chaos which visiting journalists described in hellish terms. Stampeders milled by the thousands, seeking shelter, buying provisions for the trail,

Shore

only a few aware of the labor and hardships that awaited them.

Tradesmen, professionals, merchants and con artists operated from tents and shacks, with here and there a solid building arising from the mess. Sounds of construction and countless conversations underlay a babble of curses and shouts and laughter, all mingled with the music and cries of combat pouring from jerry-built saloons and pleasure palaces.

Oxen and horse-drawn freight wagons churned muddy streets into ooze, while a young woman traveled about in a buggy

Mollie Walsh

A n engaging tale from Skagway's heyday concerns one "Packer Jack" Newman, who ran a mule train on White Pass. There he met and fell in love with Mollie Walsh, proprietor of a grub tent.

A Skagway faro dealer made the mistake of announcing his own affection for Mollie, whereupon Packer Jack shot him dead. Soon thereafter Mollie ran away to Seattle with another packer named Mike Bartlett.

Packer Jack eventually took a wife and settled down in Skagway, but his warm feelings for Mollie persisted through the years. In time, by way of expressing his unrequited love, he commissioned an artist to sculpt a bust of the departed colleen.

Jack's wife, understandably, protested—prompting him to commission yet another work of art, this one a large plaque featuring his wife's facial profile underlain by engraved words of tribute.

The plaque, for reasons unknown, became affixed to the wall of an office building in Seattle, where it remains today. The sculpture of Mollie Walsh resides little noticed in a vacant Skagway lot.

This photo was taken in 1898. The building looks the same today.

29

SOAPY SMITH

Outlaw of Skagway

enterprises as the 4th of July parade, he pacified those whom he could not intimidate. Through such a mixture of coercion and glad-handing he ruled Skagway for the first eleven months of its existence. But when a hard-working miner was blatantly robbed of a year's earnings in July of 1898, a Vigilance Committee met on a wharf to plan action against the Smith gang. Soapy approached the meeting drunk and with rifle in hand, exchanged words with Frank Reid, who had been posted as a guard, and then exchanged shots which proved fatal to both.

Within a few days Soapy's cronies had been tracked down and put aboard ships bound elsewhere.

(Frank Reid, Soapy's nemesis, was the surveyor who had plotted the street through Capt. Moore's cabin.)

A horde of thousands of strangers, representing every stripe and hue, milled about on a wilderness shore with no law or authority to guide them. It was inevi-

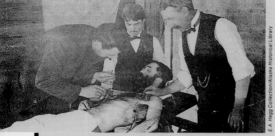

E. A. Hegg Collection/Alaska Historical Library

table that the predators among them would spot likely prey.

The predators soon found themselves under the experienced leadership of Jefferson Randolph "Soapy" Smith, an imaginative outlaw who enunciated a clear philosophy: that a minimum of good American money should escape Skagway across the passes onto foreign (Canadian) soil.

To this end Soapy and his gang swindled, robbed, extorted and murdered almost at will. By his charity toward widows, children and stray dogs, and his efforts in such civic

Case & Draper Collection/Alaska Historical Library

hitched to a tame moose. Captain Moore plunged through the scene like a man-of-war at full sail, parting the sea of humanity before him. Street vendors hawked a melange of goods and services ranging from toy balloons to dramatic performances.

People paid money to watch a sidewalk entertainer cram quantities of ceramic eggs into his mouth, while another showman led a trained bear through the streets on a leash. A man known as "Peter the Apostle" arrived from California to administer spiritual balm to troubled minds.

On the shore hastily constructed docks soon enabled arriving gold seekers to unload their gear expeditiously, but lack of money or dock space forced many to lower their baggage from ships to small boats and rafts, then slog back and forth through the shore mud until

their possessions were safely stacked on the beach above high tide line.

Horses by the hundreds, along with such animals as oxen, reindeer, goats and sled dogs, were transferred from ship to shore by means both clever and brutal, to add to the pandemonium flowing constantly between beach and townsite.

And even as they struggled toward that wilderness shore or fought through the mobs in the streets, others made their way in steady streams toward White Pass or, by boat or barge, up the coast to Dyea trading post and the Chilkoot Trail beyond.

Soapy Smith's gang

ost of those who crossed White Pass in the fall and winter of '97-'98 would later recall the experience with horror.

It was 10 miles longer than Chilkoot Trail, but its lower (by 600′) summit elevation and easier grades were touted as suitable for pack animals. So those who had shipped horses, or could afford to hire them at Skagway, were deemed to have an advantage over the mobs who must climb the steeper Chilkoot on foot, packing their own freight.

The "gradual grades" of White Pass, however, were achieved by following tortuous, zigzagging trails which corkscrewed around hills, switchbacked along nar-

row paths carved from mountain sides, crisscrossed numerous streams, and wound through boulder-strewn slopes and river bottoms.

CHALLENGE OF

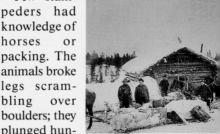

Few stampeders had knowledge of horses or packing. The animals broke legs scrambling over boulders; they plunged hundreds of feet from crumbling ledges; they fractured ribs and punctured sides against projecting edges of rock; they sank into bogs which swallowed them whole, along with their packs.

And so narrow was much of the trail that a fallen animal or other disruption of traffic sometimes forced an endless line of exhausted horses to freeze in their tracks, nose to tail, for 24 hours or more with hundreds of pounds of baggage tied to their backs.

One observer counted more than 1,000 animal carcasses during one passage over the trail. Others estimated that at least 3,000 horses perished on the White Pass between midsummer and early winter. Kind-hearted Mounties shot many of the wounded animals which survived the crossing.

Those survivors were few indeed. Journalists referred to White Pass as "Dead Horse Trail."

Men drove their beasts of burden to death, then returned to Skagway to purchase more. Novelist Jack London, a rough man with a tender spirit, witnessed the carnage. He later wrote heart-rending accounts of the rampant cruelty which swept the trail in '97 and '98.

to float down the Yukon River before winter froze them in their tracks.

Stampeders finally reach the summit of White Pass, 1898.

THE WHITE PASS

The endless traffic so damaged the pass, and the chaos became so horrendous, that movement along the route virtually halted in September of '98. The burgeoning population of Skagway swelled even further with stampeders retreating from White Pass, either to gear up for another try or to book passage on a south-bound steamer.

About 5,000 people managed to pack their freight through White Pass in '97. But only a few arrived in time

White Pass Trail/33

BUILDING THE IMPOSSIBLE R.R.

The White Pass & Yukon RR

When traffic through White Pass ground to a near stand-still in the fall of '98, an entrepreneur named George Brackett, a former mayor of Minneapolis, undertook to restore the pass by building a real wagon road to replace the disastrous horse trail. He did so that winter, in one of those feats of grueling labor and impromptu engineering that seems so miraculous for that time and place.

The old trail, widened and bridged and re-routed in many places, soon carried a stream of wagons and pack animals now handled, in many cases, by professional freight haulers. One of them was the widow Harriet Pullen, who had arrived in Skagway with $7 and a brood of children. She operated a profitable 4-horse freight outfit by day, and in the evenings baked pies for sale.

Even as road construction proceeded a Canadian group was engaged in a far grander project which would fulfill another of Capt. Moore's predictions: the laying of railroad tracks through White Pass. The project got underway in May of 1898 with more than 1,000 workers under the supervision of a colorful railroad builder named Mike Heney. The legendary Irishman had been quoted as boasting, "Give me enough snoose and dynamite and I'll build you a road to hell!"

White Pass seemed as close to hell as any railroad was likely to reach, and Heney made good his promise as his crews blasted the sides from mountains, carved roadbed from solid rock, drilled a tunnel, erected sky-high trestles, and wrestled enormous machines over jagged terrain

The railroad arrives in downtown Skagway, early 1900's.

and up towering vertical rises. In just 14 months Heney did the "impossible": he hammered a railroad through the tortuous bogs and cliffs of White Pass Trail.

By then, however, the stampede was over. On both White Pass and Chilkoot the traffic by foot, wagon and pack animal had already dwindled to a trickle when completion of the railroad ended it for good. In the meantime the irrepressible Capt. Moore had built

a dock whose operation made him a fortune. From him Mrs. Pullen purchased a large home which she converted into Pullen House, the finest hotel of Skagway's heyday.

For over 7 decades the White Pass & Yukon Railway provided a transportation link between Canada's interior and the ocean port at Skagway, although its commerce never met the high expectations kindled by the gold rush fever. As for Pullen House, it still stands today, derelict: a second-hand monument to Capt. Moore's vision, and to a thousand other dreams that would lie abandoned along the "Trail of '98."

As the doorway to Chilkoot Pass, Dyea presented a busy scene—though far less raucous than Skagway. For by the time they reached Dyea the first rush of excitement had passed for most stampeders, and they now stood poised on the brink of a trail whose hardships were common knowledge.

They knew that the Canadian Mounties, at their custom station near the summit, were requiring that each person enter Canada with a year's worth of supplies: nearly a ton.

Some brought pack animals for the first stage of the trip, although no beast could carry a load over the summit. (Livestock were, however, pushed over the divide with the intention of taking them all the way to Dawson

Ships from the West Coast, and boats and barges from Skagway 5 miles away, disgorged thousands of tons of freight on Dyea's mucky beach as stampeders organized their assault on Chilkoot Pass.

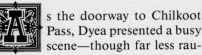

City.) Others experimented with ingenious but largely useless conveyances, including steam-powered sleds and cargo-carrying bicycles with sails.

But for the majority who must carry their freight on their own backs, the trip would consist of a constant shuttling back and forth as they moved their mountain of gear along the trail bit by bit. According to individual load capacity, they could easily travel more than 1,000 miles to and fro in order to net the 32-mile length of the trail.

Viewed from a distance, endless, undulating lines of dark shapes appeared to be crawling back and forth between clusters of white objects embedded in a sea of other dark shapes, ever in motion. The dark shapes were the stampeders with their beasts and boxes and bags, and the white objects were tents.

burdened climbers could use for a fee. (Photos of the bodies stacked single file up the stairs, in an endless chain, provide one of the most striking images from the Great Stampede.)

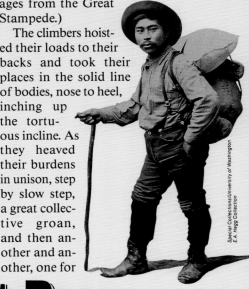

The climbers hoisted their loads to their backs and took their places in the solid line of bodies, nose to heel, inching up the tortuous incline. As they heaved their burdens in unison, step by slow step, a great collective groan, and then another and another, one for

the Chilkoot Pass

At several locations along the Chilkoot Trail there blossomed tent cities where exhausted wayfarers could procure an incredible variety of products and services ranging from plank beds to soup and haircuts and axes. The largest such community sprang up at The Scales, a bowl-shaped hollow, cluttered with boulders, at the foot of the summit. Here the stampeders paused to ponder their ultimate test.

They stared up at "The Golden Stairs"— a 40% grade rising 1,200 feet, into which an entrepreneur had carved steps which the

P.E. Larss Collection/Alaska Historical Library

each step, would echo down the valley full of watchers below. The same phenomenon was reported from the summit of White Pass.

Having attained the summit at last, they would slide to the bottom, hoist another pack, and await a chance to break into the file of climbers once more. It was estimated that the average man made 40 such trips, over a period of 3 months, in hauling his ton of gear up "The Golden Stairs."

The famous Klondike Mike Mahoney carried a piano to the summit on behalf of a troupe of female musi-

cians en route to Dawson City. But the Mounties refused to let the women pass—for their own good, they were told—and the piano eventually appeared in a small church erected near the end of the trail.

The parade continued through the

Chilkoot Trail

winter and into spring, an estimated 30,000 men and women crossing the Chilkoot Pass during the first twelve months.

Seventy feet of snow fell on the pass during the winter, and a snow slide killed nearly 70 people. But so thickly was the trail populated, Even in mid winter, that 1,000 men arrived on the scene within minutes, shovels in hand. Many victims were dug out alive, one woman twice in the same day. An ox named Mark Hanna thrashed about under the snow until he created a private cave, from which he was

uncovered in excellent health two days later.

Soapy Smith's alert representatives established a mortuary on the spot, where they unburdened the bodies of cash and jewelry before sending them on for disposition.

Such shenanigans aside, the Chilkoot presented a saga of heroic efforts performed by quite ordinary people. Except for an understandably high proportion of oddballs, the stampeders were a random cross section of the population: clerks and tradesmen, teachers and salesmen, lawyers and plumbers. Their ranks included wives and daughters accompanying husbands and fathers, and other women simply running away from home to seek money and excitement.

Crime, even murder, was not rare. But in that remote wilderness where possessions came at the cost of hard time and harder labor, thievery was treated as the worst crime of all. Law enforcement and justice, including capital punishment, were imposed by kangaroo committees—"miners' courts."

Frustration and despair were rampant. The trail today remains littered with all manner of objects—from steam engines to canoes and crates of shoes—abandoned after all the excruciating labor devoted to hauling them as far as they got. On the other hand many boats were successfully hauled the length of the route, as were freight wagons, sawmills, cook stoves and crates of live chickens.

Promoters were everywhere in the towns and trails of the gold rush, and in the spring of '98 the first tramway was under construction on the Chilkoot. By 1899 those who could pay the fee were having freight carried by tram over the summit and beyond. But the tramways and the Chilkoot Trail itself were soon rendered obsolete, first by the White Pass wagon road and later by the railroad.

A traveler on the Chilkoot in April of 1900 reported seeing only two other persons along the way. But before that happened there was still a drama to unfold between Skagway, Dyea and Dawson City.

Canadian custom house at the summit.

Did You Know?

A few stumps of piling amidst the weeds, and outlines of log foundations rotting into the soil, are all that remain now to show that Dyea ever existed. The quiet old trading post, born in 1886, exploded into a boom town of 4,000 in 1898. But when the White Pass railroad made Chilkoot Pass obsolete, Dyea quickly withered and died. Most of its structures were eventually dismantled and hauled to the young community of Skagway 5 miles away.

Miles Canyon

y the spring of 1898 about 30,000 people had crossed the two passes and now gathered in sprawling tent cities around the shores of Lake Lindeman and Lake Bennett at the foot of the mountains. From there a chain of connected lakes and rivers, eventually joining the great Yukon, would enable them to complete the journey to Dawson City entirely by water.

They passed the winter felling trees, laying bare the landscape about Lakes Bennett and Lindeman, and began the tortuous process of whipsawing moist logs into lumber for boats, barges and other craft. A few

handmade vessels, ranging from multi-ton scows to catamarans, kayaks and log rafts, slowly began to move in one great mass. Propelled chiefly by sail and oar, but also by steam engine and hand-cranked paddle wheel, the motley fleet exited the lakes.

Their initial progress over rivers and lakes was easy, after the ordeals of the mountain passes, until they encountered the hair-raising hazards

THE REST OF THE

had hauled pre-built vessels across the mountains—including Mr. and Mrs. A. J. Goddard, who somehow transported two small sternwheel steamboats, piece by piece, over White Pass.

Then, one day in May when the ice had cleared, the Canadian wilderness witnessed a sight to boggle the imagination: upwards of 7,000 mostly

of Miles Canyon. There the river was compressed into a narrow cleft between sheer rock walls. The waters roared into a giant whirlpool before spurting through a 30-foot-wide outlet from which they thundered, with the velocity of a cannon shot, into Squaw Rapids—leading in turn to a notorious stretch of white water known as White Horse Rapids.

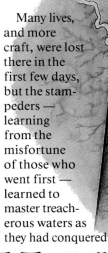

C.L. Andrews Collection/Alaska Historical Library

Many lives, and more craft, were lost there in the first few days, but the stampeders — learning from the misfortune of those who went first — learned to master treacherous waters as they had conquered

TRAIL

perilous trails. Some declared themselves river pilots and sold their services to newcomers. Still another wilderness entrepreneur appeared on the scene to construct a wooden rail tramway over which horses could pull boats and wagons around White- horse Rapids.

Meanwhile the huge fleet that had departed en masse from Lindeman and Bennett was disintegrating into the ragged configurations so common to the stampede. A broken line of vessels extended along the river all the way from Bennett to Dawson City, the craft so close that rumors traveled the length of the route like a telegram.

Then, with the worst behind and the glittering city almost at hand, the greed that goes with gold reached out to seize them. Paranoia rolled down the Yukon as partners eyed each other in con-

DAWSON

YUKON RIVER

N

YUKON TERRITORY

WHITEHORSE

BENNETT

DYEA

SKAGWAY

ALASKA

e Bennett, 1898

41

templation of the riches that lay ahead, and the distribution thereof. Frustration and fear, so long pent up, erupted among the stampeders.

It became common to see agitated men tossing bags and boxes into piles along the river bank as angry partners divided their possessions. Some sawed boats in two. Even in their rage, however, they practiced the virtues of procedure learned along the trail. The embattled travelers organized two ad hoc communities—designated Split-Up City and Split-Up Island—where they could lay out their worldly goods for equitable division. Split-Up City organized to the point that an elected mayor served to arbitrate disputes on a full-time basis.

But having survived Chilkoot and Miles Canyon, they survived this final spasm of the spirit. One day the stampeders, having rounded a bluff on the Yukon where it meets the Klondike, suddenly saw before them a veritable metropolis in the boondocks: Dawson City!

THE CITY OF GOLD

P.E. Larss Collection/Alaska Historical Library

D awson City—a conglomeration of tents, log cabins and rough-hewn frame buildings —sprawled over a stretch of wet flatland where the Klondike River flowed into the Yukon. Day after day in June of 1898 the stampeders poured into the site until their boats were tied six abreast for a distance of two miles along the shoreline.

Most newcomers were surprised to find so large a community that deep in the wilderness, but Dawson had been growing for almost two years since the original gold strike at nearby Bonanza Creek on August 16, 1896. Perhaps 2,000 prospectors, traders and drifters had been scattered through the Yukon basin at the time of the discovery, and news spreading along the river brought most of them converging on the scene.

So the arriving stampeders discovered that the good gold claims were already staked and worked even as they struggled up Chilkoot Trail and White Pass. A sizeable group of millionaires already wallowed in gold, but only a few survivors of the great stampede ever acquired enough to pay for their long and arduous trip.

At midsummer the Mounties estimated the population at about 25,000, including workers in the gold

𝒟𝒾𝒹 𝒴𝑜𝓊 𝒦𝓃𝑜𝓌?

R umors swept the nation that famine threatened Dawson City. Congress acted. Over 500 reindeer—meat on the hoof— were shipped from Norway to Alaska, with Lapland herders to drive them over the mountains and down the frozen Yukon. No famine actually existed, but about 100 reindeer survived to astonish Dawson City with their arrival in the spring of '98.

fields. Sixty sternwheelers steamed upriver from St. Michael on the Bering Sea coast that summer to unload hundreds of passengers, 7,400 tons of freight and 120,000 gallons of liquor. By August Dawson had 2 banks, 2 newspapers, 5 churches, 12 sawmills, a telephone service and a movie theatre.

A few of the newly arrived stampeders survived by plying a trade or by backbreaking wage labor in the gold fields they had hoped to own. On the sand bar along the riverfront an open-air bazaar sprang into existence as hundreds of people displayed for sale the supplies and equipment and mining tools they had packed so laboriously over the passes and

floated so perilously through Miles Canyon and Whitehorse Rapids.

Witnesses at the time described throngs of bedraggled men trudging back and forth along the streets of Dawson City, bound nowhere, eyes blank, backs bent as though the burdens of Chilkoot and White Pass still weighted them down in memory.

By August about a third of them had boarded sternwheelers headed downriver for the coast, where they could board a ship for Seattle. But even as disillusioned stampeders drifted away, Dawson City's international notoriety continued to draw newcomers who repopulated the city even as gold mining itself wound down.

Then word arrived that gold was being scooped off the beaches of Nome near the mouth of the Yukon. Dawson nearly emptied as men and women rushed to board sternwheelers bound for the new bonanza.

Southcentral Alaska

*T*he southern coast of Alaska describes a neat half-circle along the Gulf of Alaska. The area between mountains and ocean is the Southcentral region, a lively mix of wilderness and urban life, where moose, railroad train and jogger often come face to face.

© 1985 Bill Ruth / Alaska Photo

Anchorage
■ *Metropolis in the Wilderness*

I t is said elsewhere in the state that the chief virtue of Anchorage lies in its close proximity to Alaska. Anchorage people accept the jibe in good humor, for there are enough moose wandering into town, and occasional bear sightings in the wooded neighborhoods on the mountain slopes, to remind them that Alaska is very near indeed.

Warmed by the Japanese current and shielded by tall mountain ranges from arctic weather systems, Anchorage enjoys a moderate climate which, combined with its accessibility by land and water and by international air routes, has made it the economic, communication and transportation center for the state—and its burgeoning oil industry.

The Port of Anchorage handles 75% of the general cargo moving to and from Alaska. The city is headquarters for the Alaska Railroad, which the state recently purchased from the federal government. Merrill Field, a small-plane base, logs more take-offs and landings than New York's Kennedy Airport, and 10% of the float planes in the U.S. are based on Lake Hood near Anchorage International Airport—which ranks 7th in international traffic. The city leads the nation in vehicles per capita, as a crawl through rush-hour traffic will illustrate with tooth-grinding clarity.

But despite its urban character and commerce, Anchorage values and maintains its Alaskan outlook. Within the city are more than 100 parks and 80 miles of paved trails for bicyclists, joggers and skiers. A short drive along spectacular Turnagain Arm leads to a much-used ski resort, and local people join tourists in flocking to view Portage Glacier, just a few miles farther down the road.

Also popular with residents and tourists alike is a growing zoo complex, inhabited by nearly every kind of animal native to Alaska—and many birds as well.

Bordering the city is a half-million-acre state park where animals roam

Float plane traffic at busy Lake Hood seems attract the expert scrutiny of sea birds which line the shore to observe takeoffs and landin, Is it possible they really control the flow?

free and Anchorage people hike, climb, camp and ski in a wilderness of rugged mountains and valleys.

Virtually the entire city turns out for Fur Rendezvous, a 10-day community festival marking the end of winter, with more than 100 events staged by 5,000 volunteers. The celebration includes the World Championship Sled Dog Race, a 3-day event attracting contestants and spectators from around the world.

Perhaps the essence of this "City in a Wilderness" was symbolized by a recent, fleeting episode. A rare Snowy Owl perched atop a downtown church, and there it spent an entire day staring into the clouds reflected in the glass walls of the high-rise office building next door.

Anchorage Gardens

One of the most unexpected sights encountered by first-time visitors to Anchorage is the profusion of flower gardens which brighten public places throughout the city, and particularly in the downtown area. Even local people seem newly amazed each summer when their northern soil suddenly bursts forth with lush floral displays.

The rainbow of blossoms, petals and greenery is the product of a municipal program, developed over the past 20 years, which now grows

Early Anchorage History

I n 1915, on the flats of Ship Creek (site of the present-day terminal yards), a contingent of workers disembarked from a ship to organize construction of the railroad which the federal government was to lay between the port city of Seward to the south and the gold mining town of Fairbanks to the north.

By the time the railroad was completed in 1923 it was sustaining a population of 2,000 people in its young headquarters city of Anchorage. Construction of Fort Richardson and Elmendorf Field adjacent to the

city, followed by military activities of World War II—and in particular the great surge of defense construction after the war—sent the population skyrocketing to 43,000 by 1950.

The military boom was waning when oil discoveries on the Kenai Peninsula, quickly followed by

Statehood in 1959, launched a new economic era which would establish Anchorage as headquarters for escalating oil activity, a crossroads for international air traffic, and gateway for an expanding Alaska tourist industry.

The devastating earthquake of 1964 proved to be only a temporary setback. For the discovery of the immense Prudhoe Bay oil fields in 1968 led, in the 70's, to the most massive private construction project ever undertaken: the 800-mile Trans-Alaska Pipeline.

Anchorage prospered greatly from its role as administrative and supply center for that giant project, and remains today the focal point for a multitude of developments stemming from Alaska's oil production and the wealth it generates for the state.

50,000 plants to be distributed annually among 35 separate sites. Each site may contain from one to a dozen individual garden plots, and the plots are augmented by about 300 hanging baskets such as those seen along 4th Avenue and in sidewalk parks. The program also includes landscaping with a nursery stock of up to 3,000 trees and shrubs.

Gardens are designed anew each year, with seeding commencing in December in the 16,000-ft. municipal greenhouse staffed by 9 permanent employees. During the winter residents visit the greenhouse by the hundreds to relax on wooden benches while they absorb the sights and smells and warmth of the garden surroundings. The atmosphere is

The Legend of Sleeping Lady

Long before Alaska ever felt its first snowfall, the legend says, a race of gentle giants inhabited the Cook Inlet area. Among them was the maiden Nakatla, whose lover, Kudan, was sent as an emissary to make peace with warlike invaders from the north.

Nakatla awaited his return at their favorite trysting place, a quiet pool in a valley embraced by two arms of land. Her friends, come to tell her that her lover had been ambushed and killed, found her sound asleep. And so they left her, asking the gods to protect her slumber until peace returned forever to their land.

The gods complied, cloaking the sleeping lady with grass and flowers in summer, and in winter covering her with a soft blanket of snow.

She lies there still, across the Inlet west of Anchorage, easily visible from the vicinity of Resolution Park at 3rd and L. Most observers see her lying on her back in profile. But she may toss in her sleep, for others see her just as clearly lying on her side.

enhanced by the sounds and colors of a large population of birds, including parakeets, doves, quail and cockatiels, which have been living and reproducing in the greenhouse for ten years.

And come Spring, residents look forward to the floral surprise which will appear on a hillside near downtown, where each year a new image—perhaps the Alaska flag, or the Big Dipper, or a moose head—will gradually blossom and take shape in "living color."

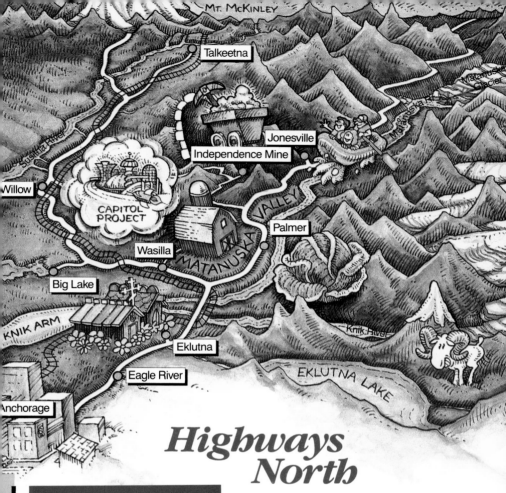

MT. McKINLEY

Talkeetna

Matanuska Glacier

Jonesville

Independence Mine

Matanuska R.

Willow

Susitna River

CAPITOL PROJECT

Palmer

MATANUSKA VALLEY

Wasilla

Big Lake

KNIK ARM

Knik River

Eklutna

Eagle River

EKLUTNA LAKE

Anchorage

Highways North

© 1985 Steve McCutcheon

*T*he road from Anchorage to Palmer, now part of the Glenn Highway, was opened to traffic in 1936. The original Glenn Highway, connecting Palmer with the Alaska (ALCAN) Highway, was descended from a hodgepodge of old trails and wagon roads which were joined together as part of a World War II highway expansion program.

The highways in the Knik Arm and Matanuska Valley areas give access to a rich blend of Alaska history: from ancient Eklutna to young Anchorage to the brand new urban strip through Wasilla; from the farmland of Palmer to the placer gold of Willow Creek to the 1930's mink farm which once operated on Nancy Lake.

Eklutna

I
t's but a short distance down the narrow access road, but it seems to move backward through a century as it comes upon the ancient Russian Orthodox church, adjoining the cemetery with graves covered by tiny "spirit houses." They lie just outside the Tanaina Indian village of Eklutna, just off the Glenn Highway about 25 road miles north of Anchorage.

Migratory Indians used the site as a winter camp; later on, Russian trappers came and went. It was also the crossroads of several old Indian trails. But not until 1923 did it become a permanent settlement which would grow into the major Tanaina community in the Cook Inlet region.

The white frame St. Nicholas church now in use replaced the original log structure in 1962. The older building, housing icons two centuries old, is believed to have been erected in the Russian mission and trading post across the Arm at Knik in 1835, then dismantled and reassembled at Eklutna in 1899. The brightly painted spirit houses reflect a blend of Tanaina culture and the Russian Orthodox faith which the Indians adopted.

Eklutna's last traditional chief, Mike Alex, who died in 1977, was the son of Alex Vasily, the last practicing shaman in the Cook Inlet area.

Were it not for the mountain ranges which enclose the Matanuska Valley on three sides, one could drive its narrow back roads, past fields of grain and herds of dairy cows, and easily imagine one's self projected into the farm country of the American Middle West.

The impression is reinforced by its principal community of Palmer, population about 2,500, whose flat terrain and low-slung architecture suggest typical scenes from a hundred small towns of the great prairies.

The valley was first homesteaded in the early 1900's, mostly by settlers who had come during the previous decade to seek gold along nearby rivers. But it remained wild and remote until 1935 when the federal government, as a measure to aid victims of the Great Depression, imported over 200 families from northern states to establish a new agricultural colony in the Matanuska Valley.

A government agency supplied the pioneer farmers with standard designs for their houses and barns; thus many buildings throughout

Matanuska Valley

the valley seem like images lifted from a farm belt calendar of the 1930's.

The economics of marketing prevented the colony from developing a self-sustaining farm economy, but farming continues on a small scale, and the Valley is famous for such heroic products as 70-pound cabbages and strawberries that could shade a plum.

Today the farm land is giving way to "suburban crawl" emanating from Anchorage. Palmer has become the seat of government for the Matanuska-Susitna Borough government, with much of its activity deriving from the presence of various borough, state and federal offices.

PIONEER FARMERS

In May of 1935 over 200 farm families from the Midwest, having been selected by the federal government to create a new agricultural colony in Alaska, had been transported north by ship and now began boarding trains in Anchorage for the final leg of their journey to the tent city of Palmer in the Matanuska Valley. There they would be provided with 40 acres of land, a house, barn and other necessities, in exchange

The Anchorage Museum

for $3,000 to be repaid over 30 years.

With winter just 5 months away, the colonists frantically set about carving roads through virgin forest, raising houses and barns and clearing acres of trees with axes and handsaws, while they somehow managed to keep their families fed, clothed and healthy (the camps were swept by outbreaks of mumps and measles during the first few weeks).

In their struggle for survival the farmers found themselves tripping over journalists and photographers arriving from all over the nation to record their drama. And they were pestered by politicans making inspection visits, for there was heated controversy "stateside" as to whether the program was an expression of American pioneer spirit or a dangerous experiment in communism.

"Cream Puff Pioneers" they were called by the critics (not, however, by anyone who had actually visited the scene). But by 1940 there were still 150 families—over 700 people—laboring to hack and pound the wilderness into productive farm land. They would have their best days just before and after World War II, when population surges related to military construction created a demand for all the food the farmers could produce.

Since the mid 1950's, however, the trend of agriculture in the Matanuska Valley has been downward. It is more economical to ship meat, eggs, produce and milk from the west coast. Livestock can still be seen grazing amidst rolling fields, but the farms usually provide only a partial source of income. Many have been acquired by land developers for housing and industry, and others await an offer too good to refuse.

The Anchorage Museum

Miners at Jonesville Coal Mine

MINING
Gold & Coal

Although the Matanuska Valley gained repute as Alaska's prime agricultural region, it has also been witness to numerous mining ventures.

Coal deposits a few miles north of Palmer were worked with marginal success—first supplying the railroad and then various military and other public utilities—until the advent of natural gas eliminated most of the market around 1967.

Gold mining fared better in the Willow Mining District which included both the Matanuska and Susitna valleys. Placer claims were first filed in 1897, and some are active on a small scale today. More significant were the hard rock mines in the Talkeetna Mountains, which began produc-

ing in 1909 and blasted millions in gold from their tunnels before World War II forced their closure.

One of the largest, the Independence, in 1940 had a payroll second only to that of the Alaska Railroad in Southcentral Alaska. Today its huge abandoned buildings loom over the mountain slopes like haunted ruins. They lie about 20 miles from Palmer within a State Historic Park off Hatcher Pass Road, which connects with the Glenn Highway.

Hatcher Pass Road—the route of a wagon trail originally built to service the gold mining operations—winds and climbs for more than 30 sometimes breathtaking miles, surmounting the Talkeetnas at 3,500 feet before descending to a junction with the Parks Highway near Willow.

Mining quartz was tough work; any sign of "color" deserved a long, loving look.

The Capital That Never Was

In 1974 Alaskans voted to move their state capital closer to population centers in Southcentral and the Interior. Two years later, voting on three possible sites, they chose a 100-acre tract of state land near the community of Willow on the Parks Highway, about 80 road miles north of Anchorage.

Residents cruised the highway bordering the site as they envisioned glass-domed edifices and spiraling walkways where herds of moose now browsed. Land prices soared.

But in 1978 the voters again asserted themselves. They approved an initiative requiring that a bond issue for the capital move must be approved in advance; simultaneously they rejected just such a bond issue, which placed the cost at $900 million.

However the move concept retained considerable vigor over the following years, as did urban growth and property values around Willow. But opponents of the move maneuvered onto the 1982 ballot a new price tag for the project in excess of a billion dollars—plus a proviso that rejection of the bond issue would automatically erase the favorable capital move vote of 1974.

Again the electorate spoke. Not surprisingly, the proposed capital site reverted to the moose.

© 1985 Steve McCutcheon

Talkeetna

Few Alaskans were less enthused about the capital move than the residents of Talkeetna, a tiny village which would have found itself on the outskirts of the teeming new metropolis. Talkeetna had been born in the early 1900's as a base for trappers and gold miners. When mining and trapping were gone it survived as a haven for independent souls, and its appearance and life style have changed little since those pioneer days. Talkeetna's 300-plus people cherish their life away from the mainstream, but cheerfully entertain tourists and enjoy the town's role as a staging center for climbing expeditions en route to Mt. McKinley, just 60 miles away.

Oil
Platforms

Anchorage

Alyeska

TURNAGAIN ARM

Hope

Portage

KENAI
MOOSE
RANGE

Whittier

Kenai

KENAI RIVER

Clam
Gulch

HARDING
ICE FIELD

Seward

Ninilchik

Homer

Seldovia

KENAI FJORDS

Highways South

*C*limbing and dip-
ping through
mountain passes and valleys,
the Seward Highway follows
pathways beaten by Eskimos and Indians of pre-history, and by Russian
trappers and American prospectors
who followed.

South of Turnagain Arm the Hope
Highway loops to the shore where
two mining towns, Hope and Sunrise, sprang to life at the turn of the
century.

The Sterling Highway meanders
south to Kachemak Bay through a
tableland once trod by Indian and
Russian hunters.

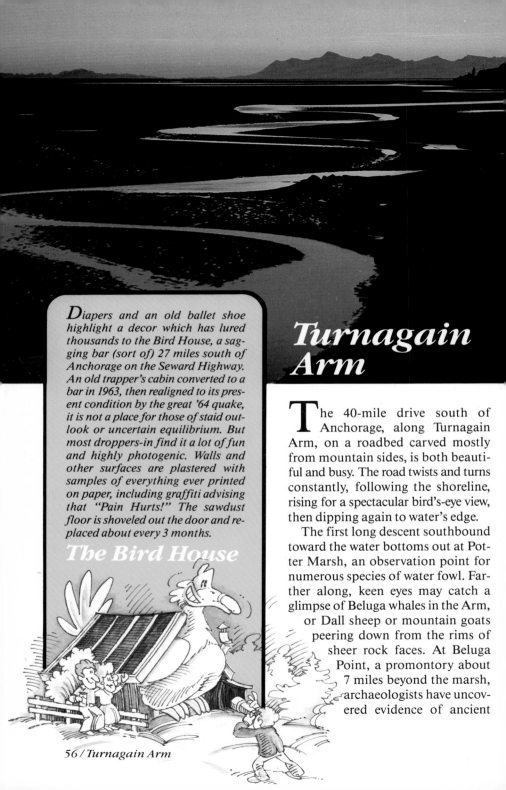

The Bird House

Turnagain Arm

The 40-mile drive south of Anchorage, along Turnagain Arm, on a roadbed carved mostly from mountain sides, is both beautiful and busy. The road twists and turns constantly, following the shoreline, rising for a spectacular bird's-eye view, then dipping again to water's edge.

The first long descent southbound toward the water bottoms out at Potter Marsh, an observation point for numerous species of water fowl. Farther along, keen eyes may catch a glimpse of Beluga whales in the Arm, or Dall sheep or mountain goats peering down from the rims of sheer rock faces. At Beluga Point, a promontory about 7 miles beyond the marsh, archaeologists have uncovered evidence of ancient

Eskimo hunting and fishing camps.

The second highest tides in North America surge into narrow and shallow Turnagain Arm, then rush out again to leave the sea bottom exposed almost shore to shore. Scene of minor gold rushes near the turn of the century, the Arm is today known chiefly for its beauty and as the gateway to Alyeska Ski Resort, Portage Glacier and the attractions of the Kenai Peninsula.

National Maritime Museum The Anchorage Museum

CAPTAIN COOK'S VISIT

Turnagain Arm was named by one of history's greatest explorers, English Captain James Cook, whose ships *Resolution* and *Discovery* entered Cook Inlet in the summer of 1778.

Cook attempted to navigate the projection of water he found off the northern tip of the Inlet, only to encounter contrary winds which turned him back again and again—hence the name he bestowed upon "the River Turnagain" now known more correctly as Turnagain Arm.

He sent a boat crew commanded by William Bligh to explore Fire Island, near the mouth of the Arm. The young officer would years later become Captain Bligh of the famous *Mutiny on the Bounty.* Also aboard Cook's ship as a marine volunteer was John Ledyard, an adventurous Yankee from Connecticut, who during this voyage became the first white American to set foot on Alaskan soil.

Cook departed disappointed that the Inlet hadn't proved to be the elusive "Northwest Passage," as he had hoped, and soon thereafter set a course for Hawaii, where he met his death.

*C*ook's log reported "a prodigious tide, it had a terrible appearance"—possibly a reference to the phenomenon called a bore tide. As the onrushing Cook Inlet tides (up to 39 feet) are squeezed into narrow Turnagain Arm, their momentum creates a wall of foaming water 2 to 6 feet high and traveling at a speed of 10 mph, as distinct as a line of charging cavalry. (Imaginative boosters of local tourism have tried, without avail, to promote an image of Eskimos and Indians racing their canoes on the crest of a bore tide, surfer-style. But skeptics throw cold water on the concept.)

Bore Tides

Alyeska
(and Girdwood)

About 10 miles beyond the Bird House is the turnoff to Alyeska Resort, the largest such facility in the state. Its downhill slopes attract skiers from other states and foreign countries (there are excellent cross country

© 1985 Nancy Simmerman/Alaska Photo

trails and glacier skiing too), but during warm months it remains popular as a casual stopover and as a take-off point for sightseers, hikers and campers.

A mile-long chairlift ride, a memorable experience in itself, leads to a mountain-top restaurant and an overwhelming view of Turnagain Arm, mountain peaks and glaciers—and clouds you may look down on.

Much of the local color centers on the adjoining community of Girdwood, which began as a mining base after prospector James Girdwood discovered gold in nearby Crow Creek in 1900. It was also a waystop on the historic old Iditarod Mail Trail connecting the port of Seward with Nome. Visitors may inspect the old buildings and even pan for gold at the Crow Creek Mine, a short drive from Alyeska.

Portage

From ancient times Eskimos and Indians, and later Russian traders, used Portage Glacier as a portage between Cook Inlet and Prince William Sound. The glacier's face in 1893 stood near the present site of the visitor's center, but in 1914 it began to retreat, leaving a lake in the trough it had gouged. The lake is now about 3 miles long and 650 feet deep. Although the glacier itself advances approximately 15 inches per day, rapid melting leaves it with a net loss of ground.

Glacier

The area is sometimes struck by hurricane-force winds which have peeled asphalt from the parking lot and toppled box cars from the railroad tracks in Bear Valley across the lake.

The wildlife in Portage Valley—through which the road passes between highway and glacier—includes brown and black bear, mountain goats, Dall sheep, wolves, coyote, moose, porcupine and numerous smaller animals.

Why the Ice is Blue

Because glacier ice has been so densely compressed by the enormous weights which form it, it is virtually devoid of cracks and air bubbles which would reflect light. The dense ice itself refracts light, separating blue from the spectrum and reflecting it while other color wavelengths are absorbed. Only the blue wavelengths reach the eye of the observer. The hues of glacier ice vary dramatically with the density of the ice and changing light conditions.

Portage & the '64 Earthquake

Between the highway and the water at the end of Turnagain Arm, near the turnoff into Portage Valley, can be seen somber evidence of the gigantic "Good Friday" earthquake which shook Southcentral Alaska on March 27th, 1964.

However the scene does not suggest a quake so much as it conveys a mood of desolate quietude: an expanse of low and soggy muskeg, spiked by the gray trunks and scraggly limbs of dead trees, with here and there the bleached-out frame of a decaying cabin sinking at cockeyed angles into the earth.

The abandoned buildings were part of the former community of Portage, which sank 10 feet during the quake, to be flooded by salt water which drowned trees and cabins alike.

The 10-ft. drop wasn't much, however, compared to occurrences in other areas. The '64 quake, centered under Prince William Sound, moved more ground farther, both vertically and horizontally, than any ever recorded save one. Its shock waves were felt 700 miles away, and it created tidal waves which drowned 10 people in California and 4 in Oregon.

In fact it was waves created by underwater disturbances which caused the most spectacular and violent effects. An undersea slide near

Port Valdez sent a wave slamming up a mountain side to topple trees 100 feet above tidewater. (During a 1958 quake near Yakutat a wave climbed more than 1,700 ft. up a mountain side, wiping it clean down to bedrock as it destroyed 4 square miles of forest.)

In the ports of Seward, Whittier, Valdez and Kodiak, large docks and warehouses—in fact, entire waterfronts—simply dropped from sight. Trains, with their locomotives, were scattered over the landscape like toys. The seaside Native village of Chenega was wiped away. Ships were left high and dry inland, like Noah's ark, far from water's edge. At one port city the ocean floor sank so abruptly that the water disappeared as down a drain, leaving an empty trough into which a towering wall of water quickly rushed to surge over the waterfront and up the mountain slopes.

The quake was recorded at a Richter Scale of 8.4 to 8.6, but recently revised calculations put it at 9.2, the strongest ever registered in North America and one of the greatest in all history. It generated 5 times the energy of the famous San Francisco shake of 1906.

An unusual and destructive feature of the '64 quake was its duration:

The Anchorage Museum

© 1985 Sam Kimura

Portage, once a quiet settlement, settled into nothing but quiet.

more than 4 interminable minutes of earth shaking so violently that people found it impossible to stand without support.

Several blocks along 4th Avenue in Anchorage sank 10 feet or more. An entire residential neighborhood slid toward the sea, its houses tossed about on earthen waves like broken matchboxes. Huge concrete walls fell into a downtown street; an apartment building under construction completely collapsed.

There was a saving grace: the quake struck at 5:36 p.m., after schools and commercial buildings had been mostly emptied. So despite state-wide property damage approaching $500 million, the loss of life was a relatively

few 131 persons (including lives lost outside the state).

And like most tragic events, it even produced a few humorous stories after the fact. An Anchorage store owner, for example, was showing a camera to a woman tourist when the first rattle shook the premises. The startled lady was assured by the manager that such temblors were common and to be ignored. A few minutes later, with the store in shambles and sounds of chaos still ringing in their ears, the tourist picked herself off the floor to exclaim, "My goodness! I don't know how you people put up with this!"

The enormous damage to property was soon erased, and after two decades even the scars from natural disruptions have been smoothed over by time, water and wind. Those sunken cabins and skeletal trees at the abandoned site of Portage are among the few reminders still visible from a public roadway.

Whittier
Alaskan
Seaport

Whittier was a tidewater landing for Indians, Russian traders and prospectors, bound for Cook Inlet via the Portage Glacier trail, until traffic was blocked by the lake which formed as the glacier began retreating in 1914. The site lay empty until the military turned it into a humming port during World War II, only to surplus the entire area, buildings and all, in 1963. Incorporated as a city 11 years later, and endowed by the state with an excellent boat harbor, Whittier has become a much-traveled gateway to magnificent Prince William Sound, and one of the most popular boating and recreational areas in the state.

Pr

Within the vast geographical expanses of Alaska are a number of localities whose particular character seems to set them apart, almost as worlds unto them-

A Trip Through
Two Mountains

In urgent need of an ice-free port in addition to Seward, World War II engineers launched a crash program to connect Whittier to the Alaska Railroad at Portage by driving two tunnels: one through a mile of rock, the other through 2½ miles.

The Magic of
ce William Sound

selves. Glacier Bay is one, Mt. McKinley Park is another. And surely one of the richest of these areas, by any measure, is Prince William Sound.

The fish canneries and fox farms are but fragments of a history whose lush fabric includes events from nearly every era or adventure in Alaska's past:

On a misty day (of which there are many in the Sound) one can visualize, emerging from behind one of the many tiny islands, a Tlingit war canoe come from the east to raid an Eskimo settlement; along these wooded shores paddled Russian fur traders, accompanied by Aleut hunters, alert for sea otter; from England and France and Spain came the sailing ships of explorers; later ships carried

Yankee whalers; the slopes along Valdez Arm echoed the shouts of gold seekers toiling toward the Klondike; Cordova rang and rattled as hard

© 1985 Steve McCutcheon

driving construction crews drove their railroad toward the renowned "million dollar bridge" across Copper River. Most recently, giant tanker ships began arriving to collect oil from the huge Trans-Alaska Pipeline

Terminal across the bay from Valdez. And all the while in the background, gargantuan Columbia Glacier has been noisily calving massive icebergs into the frigid waters—waters enlivened by whales, porpoises and dozens of other forms of sea life. Along the slopes and the shoreline can be glimpsed bear and deer, among the rich population of land animals; and the air and the water surface teem with nearly 200 species of birds.

In Prince William Sound the traveler plies a region whose mix of beauty, history and natural treasures has few counterparts anywhere in the world.

 bout 22 miles beyond Portage Valley Road, the Seward Highway meets a junction with the Hope Highway, which loops through the mountains to the north side of Turnagain Arm and then follows the shoreline to the old town of Hope.

Hope sprang from the muskeg during the two minor gold rushes to

HOPE & SUNRISE

the Turnagain area in 1896 and 1898, with perhaps as many as 200 residents at its peak. East of Hope on the mouth of Sixmile River was the neighbor community of Sunrise, established in 1895 or earlier by some of the prospectors coming into the area over the glacier crossing from Prince William Sound. As many as 2,000 people may have occupied Sunrise during its heyday as a supply center for the small mining operations which took place on virtually every stream flowing into Turnagain Arm.

The last trading post closed in Sunrise in 1919, and nothing is visible of the town today except for a cemetery obscured by undergrowth, and remnants of collapsed buildings along the vague outlines of abandoned streets. Hope survives as a woodsy retreat for elderly retired people as well as escapees from urban life, its remaining old buildings still emanating an aura of gold mining days.

Case & Draper Collection/Alaska Historical Library

Seward
Where They Catch the Silvers

I n dire danger on the storm-tossed Gulf of Alaska, a band of early Russian seafarers found a pocket of calm water on the east coast of the Kenai Peninsula. It was an Easter day, so they thankfully christened their haven "Resurrection Bay."

More than a century later a 17-year-old girl knew a different kind of joy when she hauled, from those same waters, a silver salmon worth $10,000. The one-in-a-million prize fish had been tagged by the organizers of the 1974 Seward Salmon Derby, an annual August salt water jamboree which brings hordes of fishing enthusiasts to the city on Resurrection Bay to try for thousands of dollars of prize money awarded in several categories of competition.

Competitors from around the world gather each 4th of July for another annual event, the running-climbing scramble up and down 3,022-ft. Mt. Marathon, said to be the most rugged of 5 such events held world wide.

Seward began life in 1903 as construction base for a railroad with which private investors, in an excess of optimism, hoped to exploit the coal fields of the Matanuska Valley.

The track reached Kern at the foot of Turnagain Arm before the venture folded. It was later incorporated into the Alaska Railroad.

Seward's 3,000-plus people derive their livings from a railroad dock, state ferry dock, small boat harbor, sea food processing plants, a new harbor and ship repair facility, and a range of activities related to tourism and outdoor recreation, particularly sports fishing.

What Are Those Shapes on the Inlet?

From vantage points in Anchorage, and along the Sterling Highway to Homer, are seen odd shapes which suggest ships riding at anchor on Cook Inlet, but which never move. And at night observers are sometimes puzzled by the sight of flames glowing over the water in the distance. The odd shapes are oil production platforms, over a dozen of them strung along the Inlet, and the flames are the result of "flaring" —burning off gas vented from the oil wells. The structures' earthquake-resistant design passed a major test with flying colors during the record shake of 1964.

Kenai

In 1791 Russians branching out from their Kodiak base established a fort, St. Nicholas Redoubt, in the midst of a Tanaina Indian village on the mouth of the Kenai River. Americans arrived in 1869, replacing the departed Russians, to build their own "Fort Kenay" at the same locale —only to abandon it a year later. This 2nd-oldest permanent settlement in Alaska remained isolated and quiet, entering 1950 with a population of 500 fishermen, homesteaders, trappers and miners. Then the oil discovery of 1957 instigated developments which make Kenai today, with about 5,000 residents, the largest town on the Kenai Peninsula.

Some of the richest fishing streams and rivers in Alaska —alive in season with silver, red and giant king salmon—are accessible from the Sterling Highway between the Seward Highway junction and Soldotna. So accessible are they, indeed, that hundreds of anglers, lined lined up shoulder to shoulder along river banks, try to cast in unison to avoid tangling lines. It's been called "combat fishing," and during mid summer salmon runs the local hospital stands alert with wire cutters and pliers to remove an average hook a day from fishing folk who've been snagged by other fishing folk.

© 1985 Art Wolfe / Alaska Photo

Fishing on the Russian River

Homer

Old Ninilchik

At the Ninilchik River bridge a narrow sideroad leads off toward the west. Approaching the shore of Cook Inlet it comes upon a tiny white church topped by a distinctive slim spire. Perched on a bluff overlooking the water, it seems to contemplate the silhouettes of Mt. Iliamna and Mt. Redoubt rising above the Alaska Range on the far shore. Nearby is a cemetery, and a path slopes down to an old store building and a clutch of log cabins. This image, which tends to linger, is of the Russian village of Ninilchik — an Indian word meaning "not a bad looking little place"— established in 1820 and used as an agricultural station, penal colony and trappers' base. (This "original" village is a short distance from the present day community of Ninilchik on the main highway.)

© 1985 Harald Sund

As the southbound Sterling Highway tops its final rise, poised for the descent into the town of Homer, it looks down upon a scene that, from a distance, might be taken for the French Riviera. The small coastal community lies with tall bluffs pressing against its back, facing the blue-green waters of Kachemak Bay, which opens off Cook Inlet on the immediate right and disappears from sight to the left (reaching 30 miles into the Kenai Peninsula).

From the shore near the center of town, and dominating the bird's-eye view, a slim finger of land pokes out into the bay for 5 miles: Homer Spit, the 2nd longest such formation in the world. A paved road travels its length, past gravel beaches, campgrounds and rickety buildings, then two clusters of tiny stores and shops and eating places lining boardwalks perched above the shore on pilings. Near the end of the Spit is a busy small boat harbor, an Alaska State Ferry terminal, and a variety of docks and waterfront structures.

The town proper, and especially the Spit, exudes close-up the flavor of a New England coastal town.

The original Homer was built in 1895, when miners began taking coal from the veins on the bluffs north of town and hauling it over a railroad up the Spit to ships docked near the end. Coal mining ended in 1916, but rusted wheels from that early railroad can be seen displayed outside the Salty Dawg Saloon—the weathered log cabin (much added on to) which served as a Post Office, railroad depot, grocery store and school before it became a bar in 1957. "The Dawg," whose unfettered decor suggests kinship with the famous Bird House on Turnagain Arm, becomes a sort of unofficial community center after the summer crowds have departed.

Homer survived the departure of its parent coal mines because, shortly thereafter, several families of fishermen settled on the main shore and developed such successful vegetable gardens that they attracted homesteaders.

Homer is said to have Alaska's most ideal climate. Sheltered from the north by mountains, warmed by the waters of the bay, it has moderate precipitation and seldom feels winter temperatures below zero.

© 1985 Steve McCutcheon

Seldovia

Homer Spit

Homer Spit is more than a geologic formation; it's also a drink invented by resident Hazel Heath. Having grown too much rhubarb to eat, she was inspired to combine rhubarb squeezings with the juice of cranberries, strawberries, wildberries and "anything else tasty and available." The result— Homer Spit—has recently gone into commercial production.

& Halibut Cove

Sixteen miles southwest of Homer, on the south shore near the mouth of Kachemak Bay, the village of Seldovia supports about 500 people with its fishing and crabbing fleets, seafood processing and tourism. Seldovia Bay was occupied first by Eskimos, who were driven out by the warlike Tanaina Indians in the early 1800's. Russian traders began arriving about 1865, and in 1891 St. Nicholas Church was built atop the prominent knoll it occupies today. Trade in sea otter furs thrived until the turn of the century when the sea otter had, as usual, been hunted to near extinction. Fox farming then flourished until the Great Depression of the '30's ended the vogue for fox coats and neckpieces, at which time Seldovia turned to fishing for its chief source of livelihood. Its boardwalks, beaches and old-world atmosphere make it a popular stopover for summer visitors.

East of Seldovia lies the waterfront community of Halibut Cove, site of herring salteries and fox farms early in the century, but now home for a handful of independent souls and a summer retreat for others.

Artist Diana Tillion, one of Halibut Cove's 50-or-so permanent residents, is widely known for her drawings rendered in octopus ink. Octopus, common in Kachemak Bay, are used by other locals for food and bait.

Harding Ice Field

The coast of the Kenai Peninsula reaching southeasterly from Seward, then hooking northward to Kachemak Bay, is 700 miles of wild beauty known as the Kenai Fjords. Facing the tricky waters of the Gulf of Alaska, and lying below the perimeter of the Harding Ice Field, it is difficult to approach from either sea or land. Rising from the water are mile upon mile of rock cliffs, indented with hundreds of fjords and bays into which tidewater glaciers, descending from the ice field, drop great chunks of ice amidst primeval thunder echoing between rock walls. It is possible to see thousands of harbor seals resting on the ice floes in a particular bay. The marine population also includes whales and porpoises, even sea otters—once so numerous that the Russians built a shipyard in Resurrection Bay to handle shipment of pelts from the area, only to hunt the otter to near extinction. Kittiwakes nest on the cliffs by the thousands, and an estimated 40,000

Kenai

Beyond the top of Seward's Mt. Marathon stretches one of the most awesome sights in Alaska: Harding Ice Field, 800 square miles of uninterrupted ice and snow. The field—left over from an ice cap which once covered three entire mountain ranges—is replenished each year by an enormous snowfall, the heaviest in Alaska. Its center is a circular plain, about 140 square miles, almost completely flat. Beyond the circle appear white peaked outcroppings, the tops of mountains buried under thousands of feet of ice. Over 30 glaciers descend from the mile-high field, 4 of them more than 15 miles long.

© 1985 Steve McCutcheon

Fjords

puffins inhabit the tiny, rocky off-shore islands. From a distance one can see a surprisingly lush belt of green forest, watered by drainage from the slopes above, which separates the high white vastness of Harding Ice Field from the rock faces of the fjords below. There is also the softer beauty of occasional beaches and waterfalls in sheltered coves. Here and there may be found the remains of long-abandoned gold digs, or a homestead settled long before the area was declared a national park.

Highly photogenic moose calves are seldom far from highly protective and dangerous mothers.

Valdez
Rebuilt after the '64 Earthquake

The Anchorage Museum

The earthquake of 1964 virtually demolished Valdez. Huge docks and warehouses tumbled into the ocean as massive undersea landslides swallowed the shoreline. What remained of the town was left perched on an unstable ledge which could collapse into the water in future shakes. Rather than rebuilding there, Valdez picked itself up and moved to a solid site 4 miles down the shoreline.

Ironically, the new location had been proposed as a townsite 63 years earlier. An enterprising Valdez man hoped to sell it as a terminal site for a proposed railroad through Keystone Canyon. After the rail plan folded, other proposals were made to adopt the location with its many natural advantages. But that would have meant a 4-mile move from the settlement where

Skinner Foundation Collection/Alaska Historical Library

the gold stampeders had built their tent-and-cabin city on the beach—a long haul by pack horse or dog sled.

So the town remained where it was, until the earthquake persuaded Valdez to adopt the new/old townsite it had almost acquired more than half a century earlier.

One of the most dramatic but least known episodes of the Klondike gold rush began in Prince William Sound.

The vast majority of stampeders were taking ships up Lynn Canal to Skagway and Dyea, from there crossing White Pass and Chilkoot Pass into Canada. But several thousand others responded to patriotic advertising for the "All American Route" which began at the tip of Valdez Arm. There they were dropped with their gear onto a raw shoreline, where soon arose a tent city which would eventually become Valdez.

Horses and dog teams helped haul the gold seekers and their freight six miles overland to the foot of Valdez Glacier. From there the route lay over the glacier itself and then into the interior by river.

On a map it was the shortest path to the gold fields. But the reality of the glacier crossing was horrendous; the tribulations on Chilkoot and White Pass would pale by

comparison. Burdened by back packs, dragging their freight behind them on sleds, the stampeders faced a two-month struggle over a treacherous river of ice which climbed a mile into the sky as it stretched over 20 miles into the Chugach Mountains.

The Anchorage Museum

Any step might send them crashing through a thin crust of snow concealing a deep crack in the ice, to disappear forever. One victim, alive but beyond rescue at the bottom of a crevasse, asked that a bottle of whiskey be lowered to him so that he might toast the success of his fellow seekers.

Avalanches were a constant threat; one claimed 22 lives. Another buried an outfit and a dog which, after rescuers spent three

Valdez Glacier Trail

days of digging, was uncovered alive along with the freight.

As on Chilkoot and White Pass, the pressures squeezed the best and the worst from human nature. One group of stampeders decided

to die in the attempt. Others made it back, babbling tales of glacier demons. Those who survived the glacier crossing found themselves stalled at the other end in a stark wilderness where temperatures dropped to 60 below. They suffered from frostbite and died of pneumonia.

Of the estimated 3,500 stampeders who had set out from Valdez, only about 200 surmounted the glacier to accomplish the next leg of the journey, a wild plunge down the boiling white waters of the Klutina River.

A few, having made the Klutina passage, stopped short to prospect the Copper River Valley. Only a battered handful ever reached the Klondike, to find that the gold fields had long since been claimed by others.

to abandon a man who refused to pack his share of the freight. Overhearing their plan, he shot two men and was lynched on the spot.

Some retreated toward Valdez, only

The Trans Alaska
Pipeline Terminal

Although born of the Klondike stampede, Valdez never prospered substantially from gold. But today, across the bay at the site of old Fort Liscum, stands the 1,000-acre Trans Alaska Pipeline terminal,

representing a bonanza that dwarfs the wealth from the Klondike and all the Alaska gold rushes combined.

Into the terminal's 18 mammoth storage tanks pours the entire output of the 800 miles of 48-inch pipe which delivers the oil from the great Prudhoe Bay field on Alaska's north slope—in the process crossing 3 mountain ranges and more than 800 rivers and streams, including the mighty Yukon. The tanks are each 62 ft. high and 250 ft. in diameter, with a combined capacity exceeding 9 million barrels. The pipeline, constructed at a cost of $8 billion, has a design

A single tanker of the largest type can carry more oil than the pipeline delivers to the terminal during an entire day.

So colossal is the mass of a fully loaded tanker that, traveling at a modest speed of 15 knots, it requires a distance of about two miles to come to a stop.

To assure the safety of these

Navigating the Tankers

great ships and their cargo, and particularly of the ocean water, the world's most advanced navigational expertise is employed to guide them through the narrow channels leading from the terminal to the open sea and beyond. Computers at various far-flung locations, processing information beamed from satellites, contribute to the complex communications network which plots courses and guides the gigantic ships to their destinations.

capacity of 2 million barrels per day.

In the terminal's Operations Control Center a controller, operating a console, can control virtually the entire pipeline along with the terminal itself—operating valves and pumps hundreds of miles away, even starting and stopping the entire system.

The terminal provides 4 loading berths to service the huge tanker ships, the largest of which carry a load of oil worth more than half the cost of the $90 million ship itself.

"Threading the needle" at Valdez Narrows.

COPPER RIVER AND N.W

he gold rushes to Nome and the Kondike had passed, and the big strike near Fairbanks was still to come, when a new kind of discovery focused fresh attention on Prince William Sound. Incredibly rich deposits of copper, found in the mountains east of Valdez, inspired the Guggenheim-Morgan Syndicate to construct a railroad connecting the copper country to a tidewater port. Construction got underway from Valdez in 1905.

There then arrived on the scene Michael J. Heney, "The Irish Prince," who had made himself famous by building the "impossible" White Pass & Yukon Railroad. After surveying the proposed new route, Heney recommended that the Syndicate abandon the Valdez terminus and begin construction anew from Orca Inlet near the mouth of the Copper River. However another engineer, sent by Guggenheim to evaluate Heney's findings, recommended in turn that

The "Million Dollar Bridge"

the terminus be moved instead to the port town of Katalla on the other side of the river mouth.

Rejecting Heney's suggestion, the Syndicate began construction of a huge ocean pier at Katalla. So Heney took an enormous gamble. With his own funds he began building a road-bed from his chosen port site (present day Cordova), with the intention of being first to reach the Copper River and claiming the vital right-of-way along its course.

A winter storm destroyed the elaborate pier at Katalla, vindicating Heney's judgment and leading the Syndicate to purchase his project and assign him to complete the railroad from Cordova to the copper deposits.

Constructing the breakwater at Katalla, July 16, 1907

RAILROAD

The undertaking now depended upon construction of a bridge to span the Copper River at a point where two glaciers formed a nearly insurmountable barrier. Timing was crucial, for only a completed structure could withstand the movement of ice which would soon be forming on the river.

Heney's epic battle to complete the "Million Dollar Bridge," in a race against time and winter, provided the background for Rex Beach's famous novel, "The Iron Trail." The race was won, but Heney, weakened by the struggle, died a few months before the symbolic copper spike was driven to inaugurate the railroad on March 29, 1911.

The Copper River and Northwestern Railroad (from "CR&NW" critics derived their own name, "Can't Run and Never Will") carried fortunes in copper ore from the mines at Kennecott, but a failing copper market eventually forced closing of the mines and the railroad in 1938.

W hile much of Prince William Sound was sinking during the 1964 earthquake, most of Cordova was rising 6 feet or more. But it wasn't the first time the independent and

Cordova &
The IceWorm

isolated coastal community, never connected to Alaska's road system, went its own way.

Cordova is famous among Alaskans for its annual Ice Worm Festival, a

lighthearted community celebration named in whimsical honor of the tiny black worms which actually do inhabit glaciers and other frozen environments.

The town sprang to life when Mike Heney, the railroad builder who had constructed the famous White Pass & Yukon Railway, unexpectedly chose Cordova as the port terminus for the proposed Copper River & Northwestern Railway. Until then Valdez and Katalla had been regarded as the favored locations for a tidewater loading terminal for copper ore to be hauled from inland mines.

But even as completion of the railroad was marked by the driving of a copper spike, and a prosperous future based on copper mining seemed imminent, Cordova was obsessed not by copper but coal. Dozens of coal claims in the nearby Bering River field had for years been frozen by a federal ban on coal mining. In 1911 when a ship arrived loaded with coal from Canada, it was too much for frustrated Cordovans; they dumped the coal into the sea. "The Cordova Coal Party," also dubbed "The Cordova Tea Party," made national headlines. It also made Cordova feel better.

There followed 4 decades of booming activity as a shipping port for the rich copper ore from Kennecott Mine at the end of the 194-mile railroad. When the mine and the trains shut down in 1938, Cordova moved on to a fishing and fish processing industry which still provides the basic economy for its 2,000-plus population.

When the '64 quake left much of Cordova's vital harbor area high and dry, the town rebounded with its customary energy. Today its rebuilt small boat harbor is one of Alaska's finest.

Interior Alaska

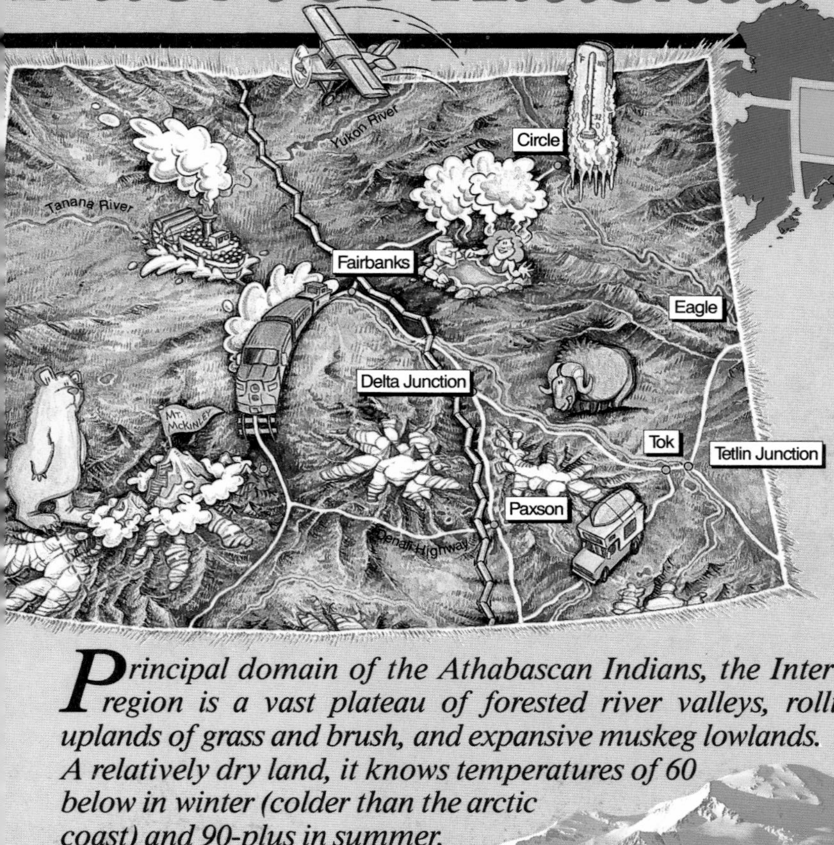
Yukon River
Circle
Tanana River
Fairbanks
Eagle
Delta Junction
MT. McKINLEY
Tok
Tetlin Junction
Paxson
Denali Highway

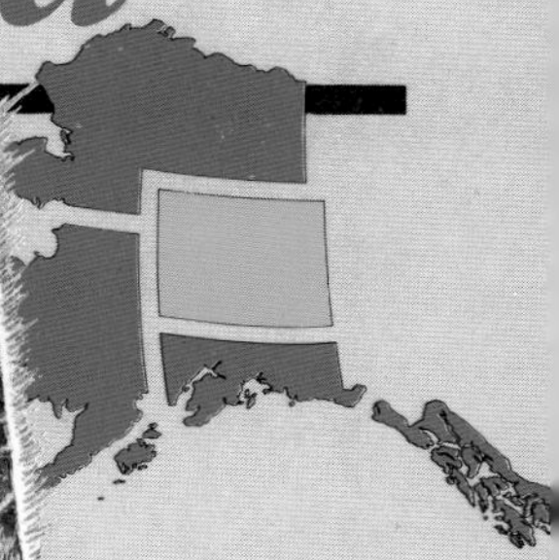

***P**rincipal domain of the Athabascan Indians, the Interior region is a vast plateau of forested river valleys, rolling uplands of grass and brush, and expansive muskeg lowlands. A relatively dry land, it knows temperatures of 60 below in winter (colder than the arctic coast) and 90-plus in summer.*

Mt. McKinley EARLY EXPLORING

Members of the 1913 expedition led by Rev. Hudson Stuck including Tatum (far left) and Karstens (third from left). Photo by Hudson S

Silhouetted against the skyline like an outsize sentry, Mt. McKinley dominates the Alaska Range, which divides Southcentral from Interior Alaska. At 20,300 feet McKinley is the highest mountain on the North American continent.

Captain George Vancouver, exploring Cook Inlet in 1794 reported sighting to the north "distant stupendous mountains covered with snow," probably the first historical reference to Mt. McKinley and neighboring Mt. Foraker. A century later McKinley remained a remote and untouched figure of mystery, the object of a worldwide curiosity fed by reports from awe-struck prospectors who came to pan the gold streams of its surrounding foothills.

It was not until *1903* that Judge James Wickersham

1903

and four companions made the first attempt to scale the mountain; they turned back at the 8,000-ft. level. Three years later Dr. Frederick Cook, a world-renown arctic explorer, claimed to have reached the summit. However numerous Alaskans doubted his story, despite the detailed account of the

This, the first of the two controversi summit flag pictures, appeared in Cook's May 1907 magazine article, labelled by him "The Flag on the Summit of Mt. McKinley."

expedition presented in his 1908 book, "To The Top of The Continent."

Declaiming his low opinion of Cook in a Fairbanks bar, miner Tom Lloyd was challenged to make the climb himself. When local businessmen offered $1,500 to finance the venture, Lloyd and three partners set off from Fairbanks in December of 1909 with a dog team, three horses and a mule.

1913

The other members of the "Sourdough Expedition" were, like Lloyd, veterans of the Kantishna gold digs near the base of Mt. McKinley. They departed clad in standard trail apparel: bib overalls over long johns, light parkas and shoepaks. Their mountaineering provisions consisted mostly of caribou meat, bacon, beans and chocolate. They also toted a 14-ft. spruce pole and 6×12-ft. flag which they planned to plant on the summit, hoping that this visible proof of success could be spotted by telescope from Fairbanks.

Three months later Tom Lloyd returned to Fairbanks announcing that all four climbers had reached both of McKinley's two peaks. The national press acclaimed their triumph. But another member of the party later asserted that only two men, Billy Taylor and Peter Anderson, had made the final ascent—and only to the north peak, which appeared higher when viewed from the Fairbanks side. Lloyd and Charlie McGonagall had waited on the slopes below.

With these conflicting claims the entire venture became as discredited as the dubious story by Cook.

Cook's account was, in fact, eventually shown to be false. But in *1913* when six men led by Rev. Hudson Stuck finally attained the true summit on the south peak (higher by 830 feet) they could see the flag pole atop the north peak—which, though lower, is actually more difficult to climb.

Nineteen years passed before another expedition stood again on the summit. That same year, *1932*, famed bush pilot Joe Crosson made

Pilot Joe Crosson makes the first plane landing, April 25, 1932.

1932

the first plane landing on one of McKinley's glaciers. His daring feat heralded the era when climbing parties would alight on the mountain side from airplanes, to be supplied by air drops summoned by 2-way radio, as they ascend the steep slopes up which the Sourdough Expedition trudged with its back packs and flag pole.

*Early climbers followed
this glacier route toward
Mt. McKinley's slopes.*

*Tundra retains heat,
keeping temperatures
20 to 30 degrees warmer
than the air above,
enabling upwards of
400 plant species to
survive Denali Park's
long, brutal winters.*

Alpine Bear Berry (right)

Denali
National Park & Preserve

Mt. McKinley

The heart of Denali National Park & Preserve consists primarily of a great alpine valley lying between the slopes of the Alaska Range and the foothills which parallel it to the north.

Few wilderness areas on earth remain so pristine and yet accessible. It is a virtually self-contained wild domain in which more than 35 species of animals, 130 species of birds and hundreds of plant species sustain themselves by completely natural processes, unaffected by human presence.

It was this special character of the area—an enclave of primeval terrain supporting a remarkable concentration of wild creatures —which led Congress in 1917 to create Mt. McKinley National Park. The Alaska Lands Act of 1980 enlarged the park to its present 6,000,000 acres and changed the name to Denali, the name, meaning "Great One," given to Mt. McKinley by Alaska Indians.

A single narrow road, completed in 1937, undulates through the rolling tundra and claws its way along precipitous rock faces to reach 90 miles into the park. Private vehicle traffic is strictly limited; most visitors view the scenery and wildlife from scheduled buses. Hikers and campers may leave the road only on foot and unarmed. Thus the role of humans is that of observer, not participant, leaving the wildlife to come and go according to instinct and the turns of nature.

Since nature follows its own rhythm, a round trip over Denali Park's road, spectacular for its scenery alone, may yield

© 1985 Tom Walker / Alaska Photo

© 1985 Steve McCutcheon

© 1985 Ken Kollodge

© 1985 Steve McCutcheon

only a glimpse or two of animal life. But it can also reveal the creatures in breathtaking array or, on rare but unforgettable occasions, provide witness to the stark drama of a wolf pack circling a giant moose, or a pair of grizzly cubs nervously watching their mother down a straggling caribou.

An occasional voice is heard to opine that a proper park should offer such amenities as paved parking areas, picnic facilities with concession stands, and a hotel with a hair salon. But Denali Park's raw and awesome wilderness, thriving under the lofty gaze of Mt. McKinley, remains Alaska's foremost attraction for visitors and residents alike.

Denali Park grizzlies, feeding mostly on roots and berries, are small compared to the 1,200-lb.-plus giants of the same species on Kodiak Island and the Alaska Peninsula, where they gorge themselves on fat salmon. But grizzly-watchers in Denali Park should be mindful that a 600- to 800-pounder can swat a moose to the ground.

No human (or animal) should ever appear to intrude on a grizzly. And if the bear can see you, hear you or smell you, it may decide you're intruding. Split decisions automatically go to the grizzly.

Denali Park / 85

The *Great Alaska Mosquito*

The journals of early explorers and sourdoughs are rich with laments over the ferocious attitude of that monarch of northern skies, the Great Alaska Mosquito *(Stingus irritadus)*. There are, in fact, more than three dozen species of the flying critters devoted to spreading misery throughout their domain.

So savagely do they press their attacks, and in such numbers, that herds of caribou have been witnessed charging wildly in circles, churning the tundra

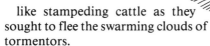

like stampeding cattle as they sought to flee the swarming clouds of tormentors.

On the bright side, the problem could have been twice as bad but for the designs of nature: only the female mosquito draws blood, which is employed in the production of eggs. (No one appears interested in asking *how*.)

An obscure sourdough legend relates how the first explorers in Alaska were facing a winter of starvation when, one late November day, a band of Indian hunters appeared lugging carcasses of newly bagged mosquitoes, dressed out and ready for roasting. The grateful explorers so relished the meat (drumsticks in particular) that they vowed always thereafter to celebrate that day of feasting as a holiday, by way of expressing thanks. But the custom never truly caught fire.

More recent is the World War II report of a Japanese pilot in the Aleutians who returned to his carrier with a disturbing tale. Flying a low reconnaissance run over Adak, his plane had been set upon by swarms of fighters of a radical new design, distinguished by flapping wings and a buzzing noise which set his teeth on edge. Curiously, the strange

Avoiding the Great Alaska Mosquito

For anyone venturing off the road and into the boondocks from April to September, a proven insect repellant and/or head net are helpful accessories.

Other Less Useful Hints:

It has been established that mosquitoes prefer the blood of blondes to that of brunettes. Toss a suitable wig into your handbag.

Because mosquitoes prefer moist, still air, you may seek relief by an occasional run to a cool, windy mountain top. Or create your own wind (technically an "apparent wind") by running in circles and making noises like a herd of caribou.

Hold a mirror to the face of an attacking mosquito. Alternatively, drive a stake through its heart.

Remember: hundreds of thousands of visitors have toured Alaska without spotting a live mosquito. Should you become one of the exceptions, take pride in the distinction.

craft seemed less intent on shooting him down than on siphoning his gas tanks. But the story is suspect. Only the Great Alaska Mosquito fits the pilot's description of his attackers, and the Aleutian Islands are one of the few parts of Alaska almost devoid of the beasts.

Whatever the truth of these and numerous other accounts, there is a group of hard-bitten Alaskans who itch to see the Great Mosquito declared the state's official bird. They cite the imposing profile of the mosquito, with its sleek snout and soaring wings, as contrasted with the rather sluggish outlines of the current official Alaska bird, the ptarmigan—which, one must admit, has inspired little prose in the journals of explorers or the files of the Japanese navy's air men.

Their idea may or may not prevail. But certainly there are few sights more impressive than the regal head of a Great Alaska Mosquito mounted in majestic repose over the flicker of a fireplace, its piercing eyes seeming still to be ablaze with fury.

© 1985 Steve McCute

The Alaska R.R.

The Alaska Railroad's kaleidoscopic journey through the heart of Alaska begins at the city of Seward, one of the most scenic ports in the world. Proceeding northward the roadbed climbs 694 feet to pass through the Kenai Mountains, then dips and rolls its way to Grandview, where it begins an abrupt descent to the shore of Turnagain Arm.

The tracks follow the shore to the main yards in Anchorage, then meander around Knik Arm to the Matanuska Valley before settling into a path following the Susitna River.

The entire railway offers frequent sightings of wildlife, but here it crosses an area in which, during winter time, beast and train conflict. Giant moose, after floundering through belly-deep snow, discover the easy going along the plowed-out tracks. But flanked by walls of snow, and unaccustomed to yielding right-of-way, the 1½-ton moose are given to fatal confrontations with encroaching locomotives. (The meat is donated to needy Alaskans.) One more fortunate moose stepped from a snow bank onto a flat car to find itself en route to distant browse.

Beyond this flatland

Now a quiet town, Nenana was once a bustling river terminal where rail freight was transferred to river boats for delivery up the Tanana and the Yukon.

From Nenana the railroad winds through flat terrain and low rolling hills to Fairbanks, just short of 500 track miles from Seward.

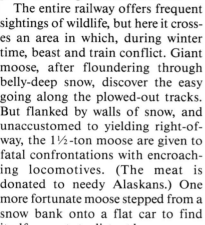

the track begins a gradual rise to 2,363-ft. Broad Pass in the Alaska Range, then winds 38 miles through the mountains to Denali National Park station. Beyond the park it snakes along the walls of spectacular Healy Canyon before descending to a wide muskeg plain stretching to Nenana at the confluence of the Nenana and Tanana Rivers.

Did You Know?

Years ago a moose, leaping onto the tracks and struck by a locomotive, fell against a switch stand and threw the switch, derailing two locomotives and several cars. (Switching equipment was quickly redesigned to prevent such accidents.)

Alaska Railroad Construction

Bedazzled by the stories of wealth emanating from Canada's Klondike, Americans at the turn of the century itched to develop their own northern territory of Alaska. They knew from experience that railroads are the key to a frontier. And so, after numerous private ventures had failed for a variety of reasons, Congress authorized the president to construct a railway from a southern Alaska port to the waterways of the interior and to such deposits of gold or other minerals as might be found.

A route from Seward to Fairbanks having been selected, men and supplies began arriving at Ship Creek, the future site of Anchorage, in 1915.

For America's experienced railroad builders it was not a particularly difficult project, except for the bridge over Hurricane Canyon and the 701-ft. span over

Alaska Railroad Collection/Alaska Historical Library

Placing the final connections on the Hurricane Gulch Bridge in 1921

the Tanana River, the largest such bridge in the U.S. at that time.

By 1917 short sections of line were operating north and south from the Anchorage construction base and between Seward and Kern Creek at the foot of Turnagain Arm. But World War I drained the project of men, money and supplies, and it was not until July of 1923 that President Harding arrived to drive the golden spike near the north end of the Tanana Bridge, symbolizing completion of the line from Seward to Fairbanks.

Admiral Hugh Rodman, a member of the President's entourage, sternly warned his companions to wear heavy winter clothing, galoshes and—in a charming non-sequitur—leggings to fend off mosquitoes. But as the Presi-

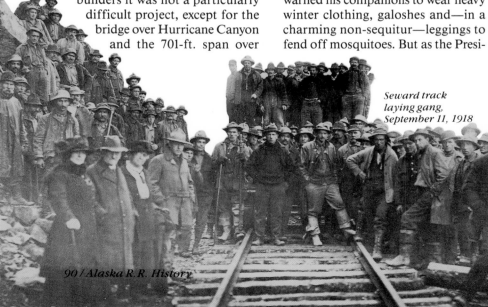

Seward track laying gang, September 11, 1918

dent addressed a Fairbanks crowd in 94-degree temperature, 3 spectators collapsed from heat prostration.

The incident nicely foretold the misconceptions which would haunt both Alaska and its railroad for years to come. A 1922 Rand McNally guide encourages tourists to enjoy "the people's railroad," but added that dog teams would always provide the backbone of Alaska's transportation system.

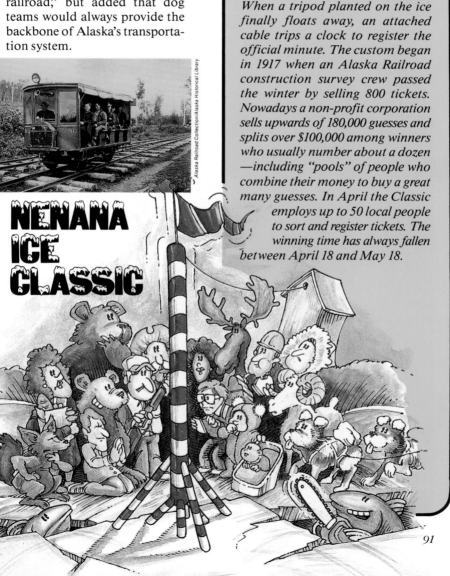

Alaska Railroad Collection/Alaska Historical Library

With all its colorful history as a bustling riverboat and railroad terminal, Nenana is famous among Alaskans chiefly for its *Nenana Ice Classic*—an annual guessing game in which residents of the state try to choose the exact date and time when the Tanana River ice will break in spring. When a tripod planted on the ice finally floats away, an attached cable trips a clock to register the official minute. The custom began in 1917 when an Alaska Railroad construction survey crew passed the winter by selling 800 tickets. Nowadays a non-profit corporation sells upwards of 180,000 guesses and splits over $100,000 among winners who usually number about a dozen —including "pools" of people who combine their money to buy a great many guesses. In April the Classic employs up to 50 local people to sort and register tickets. The winning time has always fallen between April 18 and May 18.

NENANA ICE CLASSIC

Watching the ice break up, April 30th, 1907

Charles Bunnell Collection / University of Alaska Archives

here is a special essence about Fairbanks, a crisp feeling of frontier independence. It is a spirit born of the unlikely events which unfolded on an August day in 1901 on a remote bank of the Chena River.

There, 600 miles into the Alaska wilderness, stood a seasoned con man named Elbridge Truman "E.T." Barnette with his wife, Isabelle, and a small band of men. They had been en route from St. Michael, near the mouth of the Yukon River, to the tiny outpost of Tanacross on the Tanana River, where Barnette intended to establish a trading post.

© 1985 Malcolm Lockwood / Alaska Photo

But their chartered steam boat had bumped to a stop in a shallow stretch of the Tanana. Attempting to detour via the Chena River, they again ground to a halt.

The boat captain was eager to return to St. Michael before winter closed in. Rather than retreat with the steamer, Barnette opted to unload his cargo and entourage on the river bank, there to improvise a plan of action. They were milling about, sur-

Temperatures of 100 degrees in summer and 60 below in winter have made optimists of Fairbanks people: they know that relief is never far away.

FAIRBANKS

rounded by several tons of trade goods, when out of the forest materialized their first customers.

From a hill 15 miles to the north, prospectors Felix Pedro and Tom Gilmore had spotted the smoke from the boat. They came now hoping to obtain provisions, and having done so disappeared back into the wild. It was a fateful encounter.

Barnette's crew erected an impromptu trading post of two log structures and several tents. He bided his time trading for furs with Indians who occasionally happened by, meanwhile planning his next move.

It came in March when the Barnettes, with 3 companions, loaded the furs aboard dog sleds and departed for Valdez—a remarkable trek through 400 miles of muskeg, forest and mountains, in temperatures of 40 below. From Valdez they sailed to Seattle, where Barnette purchased a shallow-draft river boat which he shipped to St. Michael in pieces.

The re-assembled vessel, Barnette and Isabelle aboard with new supplies, churned upriver to arrive at his lonely trading post in August. There was uplifting news. Felix Pedro had struck gold just 12 miles away—a discovery which virtually emptied Dawson City and Nome as hundreds of miners and boomers converged on the new bonanza to seek their fortunes.

One of the largest fortunes would go to E.T. himself, who sold his trading post at a handsome profit, staked dozens of claims in the name of distant relatives, and opened a bank. His pile of goods on the river bank would

Why is the Water so HOT?

Thermal hot springs are found throughout Alaska, from Southeast to the Interior to Nome.

A packtrain prepares to depart for Valdez in 1908.

blossom into the City of Fairbanks, with E.T. Barnette serving as both Mayor and Postmaster.

But Barnette's wheeling and dealing led to a series of financial scandals which snapped his long streak of luck. In 1911 he and Isabelle stole out of town in the middle of the night, hidden in the bed of a freight sled. He was later burned in effigy.

Subsequently he was glimpsed in scattered locales, including the huge Mexican plantation he had acquired during his heyday. But after a few years he disappeared to meet a fate unknown.

Although Fairbanks rebelled against the roguish ways of its founder, the city today recalls him somewhat fondly, and still retains that aura of vigor and optimism which he bequeathed it.

They occur where surface water seeps down to come in contact with rocks heated by the earth's molten layer, far underground. Where such ground water is trapped under a layer of impervious material, pressure created by the weight of higher levels of water drives the heated water to the surface through faults or cracks. Water usually reaches the surface at temperatures between 100 and 150 degrees F.

During the gold rush heyday of Circle City on the Yukon River, miners often spent their winters in an unlikely pastime: soaking in the steaming water of Circle Hot Springs, 40 miles away. Chena Hot Springs, 60 miles from Fairbanks, eased the bodies and minds of other sour-

ALASKAN HOT SPRINGS

doughs. (At times they could reach the water only by hacking away the ice which accumulated on the tents erected over the pools.) Today a large open pool at Circle Springs and an enclosed pool at Chena Springs are the focal points of year-round commercial resorts where frost-bitten Alaskans melt away the stresses of Interior winters.

The
Northern

Some residents of the far north, where the Aurora Borealis may be witnessed more than half the nights of the year, believe the Northern Lights make swishing sounds. Eskimos and Indians, like native people in other parts of the world, have claimed that the Aurora responds to certain sounds and movements. Whatever science may say, the Northern Lights convey a sense of mystery and awe.

They may sweep the night like multi-tinted searchlights, or roll like draperies unfurled against the sky, undulating and shimmering in profound cascades of color. They sometimes surge. They ricochet. They can flash like lightning, or flare and fade in rhythm, each change of intensity triggering a hue never seen before.

Mystical Lights

But ultimately they beggar mere words: a spectacle never forgotten and never adequately described.

Commentator Lowell Thomas once broke into uncontrollable laughter as he told his radio audience of a man who was questioned by police after neighbors reported his cavorting about the yard flapping a bed sheet. The fellow explained he was testing a technique for generating Northern Lights, a concept which so amused Thomas that he was unable to complete his report. (Early Eskimos sought to attract the Aurora by whistling, while a group of Alaska Indians sought the same result by beating on metal pans.)

Northern Lights / 97

The Anchorage

Fairbanks · Tok · Dawson · Whitehorse · Anchorage · Skagway · Haines · Valdez · Prince Rupert · Dawson Creek · Prince George · Edmonton · Calgary · Vancouver · Seattle

T he Alaska Highway swoops, climbs and wends its way through 1,500 miles of tangled and craggy wilderness once known only to a handful of sourdoughs who penetrated it step by arduous step.

Its construction was a monumental effort instigated by the need to strengthen the military defenses of northwest Canada and Alaska in the face of Japanese expansion leading to World War II.

The Anchorage Museum

In March of 1942 U.S. Army Engineers, whose number would peak at 4,500, established base camps scattered along the route and began working toward each other. In a few cases they could follow beaten paths: a wagon road, a couple of trails worn by prospectors and trappers. Elsewhere they made guesses based on aerial photos, climbed trees to spot likely directions, or sought advice

The Alaska

from Indians and other old timers who knew the territory.

Photos of the project suggest a boondock version of Dante's Inferno: workers' faces swollen with mosquito bites and caked with mud; giant machines disappearing into bottomless bogs; haggard troops in a chow line, re-

sembling snow men holding tin plates.

They died from exposure in the 50-below temperatures; a raft overturned to drown eleven men. Fatal accidents were inevitable as bulldozers thrashed through canyons of muck, chewed through tangled forests and clawed their way up impossible inclines.

Nevertheless in 8 months of struggle they built a road with 133 bridges totaling 7 miles in length, and 8,000 culverts totaling 50 miles. No sooner was their pioneer trail completed in October of 1942 than dozens of contractors with an aggregate work force of 16,000 civilians moved in to widen it and lay gravel, improve the alignment and construct more permanent bridges—a job, under conditions almost as difficult and hazardous as the original construction, which they completed in another year.

Highway improvements have been underway since the end of the war, and today most of it it paved (although conditions vary widely)

except for stretches of well-maintained gravel surface.

From the flat farmland surrounding Dawson Creek, British Columbia, the highway eases into the foothills of the Rocky Mountains at Fort Nelson, tops the range at Summit Lake (elev. 4,250 ft.), descends to follow rivers and valleys from Watson Lake to Whitehorse in the Yukon, then skirts the north side of the St. Elias Range to enter the Tanana Valley leading into Fairbanks.

It surely offers one of the most diverse and awe-inspiring cross sections of natural splendor in the world.

Highway

Arctic & Western Alaska

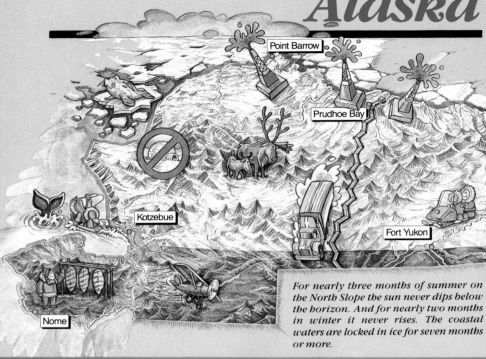

Point Barrow

Prudhoe Bay

Kotzebue

Fort Yukon

Nome

For nearly three months of summer on the North Slope the sun never dips below the horizon. And for nearly two months in winter it never rises. The coastal waters are locked in ice for seven months or more.

*O*f all the far-flung lands inhabited by Eskimo people, the North Slope section of Arctic Alaska probably comes closest to the storybook image.

© 1985 Harald Sund

Land of the Midnight Sun & Land of the Eskimo

The Arctic area as a whole is separated from the Interior region by the Brooks Range, which extends westward from the Canadian border for 600 miles across northern Alaska. On the north flank of the range, 10,000-ft. peaks ease into rolling hills which decline into a treeless tundra plain — called the North Slope—reaching 250 miles to the shore of the Arctic Ocean.

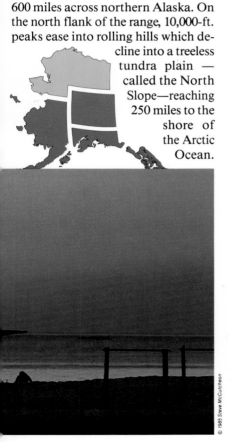

© 1985 Steve McCutcheon

For most of the year a blanket of snow spreads farther than the eye can see, so uniform that one can barely discern the line between frozen land and frozen sea. But the snow cover is thin, for precipitation is so low (5″ to 10″) that the same conditions at lower altitudes would produce a desert. And the meager fall of moisture lies trapped on the ground, because the soil is permanently frozen from a few inches below the surface to depths of hundreds of feet. The summer melt reveals huge areas festooned from horizon to horizon with countless small lakes and ponds.

A small band of Eskimos, once nomads who followed the caribou herds, has settled into a community in Anaktuvuk Pass in the Brooks Range. Most other North Slope Eskimos are whale hunters who live at Barrow and other smaller villages scattered along the coast to the west.

Temperatures here are milder than in the Interior, but unceasing north winds create deadly chill factors as low as minus 100 degrees.

Near Alaska's west coast the Brooks Range tapers down into low mountain ranges and hills which fan west toward the sea and south into the area described here as Western Alaska. Some Eskimos moved inland to occupy the river valleys, where they traded and fought with Athabascan Indians in the eastern part of the area.

Coastal or inland, they knew a somewhat easier lifestyle than their North Slope Cousins, with more snow but milder temperatures and a greater bounty of fish and game.

For thousands of years the Eskimo people thrived on what the harsh land and the frigid seas could provide. Today their society is an ever-changing composite of deeply embedded tradition mixed with elements of the white culture which presses upon them. Ocean barges and air transports now bring them packaged foods and fabricated products from distant factories. But like other Americans who keep candles in the closet and dried food in the basement, the Eskimos stick close to fundamentals, just in case technology proves less durable than their own well-tested ways.

For coastal Eskimos whales and whale hunting hold a deep cultural and psychological significance seldom comprehended by outsiders whose immediate forebears never relied upon whale meat for survival. Eskimo leaders almost invariably arise from the ranks of whaling captains, as have the first four mayors of the North Slope Borough.

Whaling villages await the spring arrival of migrating bowheads (monsters of 40 ft. and

© 1985 Steve McCutcheon

Subsist
W

The Hunt

Eskimo whalers paddle after their quarry in umiaks, boats made of animal hides stretched over a wood frame. So seaworthy are the vessels that 19th century whalers from New England often preferred the umiaks to their own famous New Bedford whaling boats.

Some modern whalers bend tradition by using harpoon guns developed in the 1800's, but others still make the first strike with hand-thrown harpoons.

Whaling, like most Eskimo undertakings, is a cooperative venture. Other boats hurry to a struck whale to help dispatch it as quickly as possible and prevent it from escaping wounded. Bowheads can reach a length of 60 feet, and an occasional boat is overturned, and its crew sent flying, by the flip of a giant tail.

more) with the anticipation other Americans exhibit toward Christmas or the Super Bowl. The entire population flocks to the shore to haul the whale carcass onto the beach, where meat is distributed among the villagers in a great celebration, with feasting, dancing and exuberant socializing.

The Eskimos voluntarily limit their kills to accord with international agreements, but the hunt itself is no less meaningful to them today than it was five hundred years ago.

The chase climaxes weeks of waiting on the beach, in the shelter of overturned umiaks, for the first sight of a whale surfacing in an offshore lead—a narrow channel of water opened as the ice breaks in spring. The bowheads migrate annually along the north coast, en route to summer feeding grounds in the eastern Beaufort Sea.

Arctic Wildlife

Although not densely populated with wildlife, the Arctic and Western regions are home to a wide variety of creatures. Caribou are most numerous. Grizzlies wander the Brooks Range and the western hills, as do a few moose. Dall sheep also inhabit the Brooks. Polar bears prowl the north and northwest coasts and offshore ice packs. Other species include the wolf, lynx, fox, hare, beaver, marmot, mink, weasel, shrew, lemming and vole. Musk-ox have been transplanted to the arctic and other areas.

Will Rogers Memorial

The descent of technology into the midst of ancient Eskimo culture was poignantly foretold by an event which occurred in the summer of 1935. It had been just 51 years since Charles Brower, a salty whaler, had established a trading post and whaling station at Barrow, to become its first white resident. Now, 12 miles down the coast, *a small group of Eskimos watched a floatplane land near their hunting camp. They talked briefly with its two occupants, who asked the direction to Barrow. The plane lifted, stalled, and crashed into a shallow lake. David Brower, son of that whaling ship sailor, helped remove the body of Wiley Post, a famous pilot on a round-the-world flight. His passenger was cowboy humorist Will Rogers, America's most beloved entertainer, whose death stunned a nation to whom the land of the Eskimo seemed more remote than the dark side of the moon.*

Barrow is the focal point of whaling tradition on the North Slope. **Nulukataq,** *the celebration of a successful hunt, includes the blanket toss, said to have originated as a way of lofting hunters above the flat landscape to spot game. A moderate toss is safe enough for amateurs, but only experienced tossees should aspire to the maximum altitudes which the procedure is capable of achieving.*

Barrow Whaling Capital of the Arctic

Barrow, the farthest north point on the continent, is one of Alaska's two largest Eskimo communities and contains the ultra-modern headquarters for the North Slope Borough, geographically the largest locally governed area in the U.S. The first generation of Eskimo swimmers is splashing in the pool of Barrow's multi-million-dollar ·school, which was financed by the Borough's enormous oil-based income and would do justice to any major American city. The Borough has also generated modern housing developments for Barrow, as well as other villages, but much of the town remains from days when lumber was almost nonexistent and houses made of scrap wood replaced traditional dwellings of sod. The names of many prominent Barrow families descend from whalers and traders who began arriving more than a century ago, including Charles Brower, who settled there in 1884 to establish a trading and whaling station.

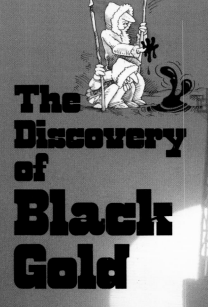

The Discovery of Black Gold

North Slope Eskimos of old, happening upon lumps of congealed black goo lying on the tundra, could never have dreamed that the strange substance would one day revolutionize their ancient way of life.

In 1886 a navy exploration party discovered specimens of oil on the Colville River near Prudhoe Bay. Then in 1914 a white teacher at the Eskimo village of Wainwright traveled 500 miles by reindeer-drawn sled to investigate rumors concerning a black lake. On a hillside he found "two living springs of what appears like engine oil" which trickled down to form a pool of oil. Both government and industry showed intermittent interest in the area during the decades that followed, and finally, in 1968, an exploratory well designated Sag River State No. 1 confirmed the presence of a major oil deposit at Prudhoe Bay.

The problem of transporting the oil to an ice-free port was solved by designing the largest construction project ever undertaken by private industry: the Trans-Alaska Pipeline. But the start of construction was preceded by

Building Ice Islands

The shallow waters of the Beaufort Sea, bordering the North Slope of Alaska, have lately become dotted with miniature islands.

The new-born islands are man-made, and each one is occupied by an oil drilling rig. They represent an innovative solution to the problem of drilling offshore in waters which are dominated most of the year by moving masses of ice capable of crushing even the sturdiest steel drilling platform.

Island construction begins in midwinter as tanker trucks spray layer upon layer of water along a route between a gravel pit and the shore, until a roadbed of ice has developed to a thickness of 2½ to 3 feet. Special rigs then work their way from the shore toward the future island location, augering through the ocean ice in order to pump sea water onto the surface. The highway of layered ice thus created sinks of its own weight until, at a thickness of about 8 feet, it becomes rigid enough to support the weight of bulldozers, road graders and the huge trucks which will haul gravel to build the island.

Specially designed machines then cut giant blocks of ice from the frozen sea, creating holes through which an endless procession of trucks dumps a million cubic yards of gravel into water typically 40 feet deep. Eventually a gravel island rises above the surface, its base on the ocean floor larger than that of a great Egyptian pyramid.

The process is a race against the summer melt, which briefly opens a narrow band of water along the coastline. During that time barges haul the drilling rig itself to the island, in section weighing up to 450 tons each. Several such rigs have struck oil, making the tiny islands some of the most productive pieces of real estate in the world.

years of planning and preparation. For 3 summers the University of Alaska, under contract to the builders, scoured the route for archeological sites which might be obliterated by construction. They found and excavated 90, up to 13,000 years old, which made invaluable contributions to the understanding of Alaska's prehistory.

Engineering and design challenges were enormous. The oil, reaching the surface at 175 degrees and flowing through the pipeline at 145 degrees, could melt the frozen ground which underlies 80% of the route, causing the

© 1985 Christopher Arend / Alaska Photo

© 1985 Steve McCutcheon

The above-ground design also helped meet the threat of earthquakes; the line passes near 4 earthquake fault lines, one of which it actually intersects. The elevated pipe lies on cross beams over which it can slide freely. And the pipe is also laid in a zig-zag pattern which sometime puzzles aerial observers but allows the line great flexibility of movement.

In places the pipe is sufficiently high to allow passage of migrating caribou, numbering about 450,000, across the North Slope. In one instance a road and a construction camp were relocated in order to avoid encroaching on a nesting area for rare peregrine falcons.

To convert this complex design into an 800-mile pipeline a work force of thousands, peaking at 21,000, converged on Alaska from all over the U.S. They would labor for 3 years, in temperatures ranging from summertime 90's to minus 80 in winter.

Commencing in April of 1974 they would drive, heave, hoist and ease their pipeline through a spectacular succession of obstacles offered by virtually every natural feature Alaska can provide. They first crossed the vast expanses of tundra on the North Slope, then clawed their way up 4,800 vertical feet to cross the Brooks Range through Dietrich Pass.

Descending to make a 2,290-ft. crossing of the mighty Yukon River, they then worked toward another great climb, through the Alaska Range. The noises of

pipe to sink and rupture. That problem was met by elevating 400 miles of the line above ground; in other areas the line was underlain with pipes through which refrigerated brine is pumped constantly, thus preventing the permafrost from thawing.

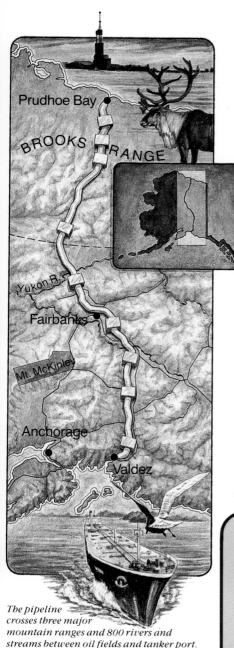

The pipeline
crosses three major
mountain ranges and 800 rivers and
streams between oil fields and tanker port.

© 1985 Nancy Simmerman / Alaska Photo

their passage blended with faint echoes of history in Isabel Pass, named for the wife of E.T. Barnette, the rambunctious founding father of Fairbanks, who struggled through the pass with his wife on that amazing wintertime trek from Fairbanks to Valdez in March of 1902.

At Thompson Pass in the Chugach Mountains, just before the pipeline drops to tidewater at Valdez, they anchored their bulldozers with steel cables as the giant machines inched huge sections of 48″ steel pipe down the seemingly impossible slopes.

The completed 8-billion-dollar pipeline occupies only 12 of Alaska's 586,000 square miles, but its flow has not only financed a multi-billion-dollar series of capital improvement programs but has given the state a "Permanent Fund" savings account exceeding 7 billion dollars.

Did You Know?

Alaskans celebrated the 1977 completion of the pipeline by contriving a game, inspired by the annual Nenana Ice Pool, in which individuals bought tickets entitling them to register a guess as to the precise minute the first oil would reach Valdez from Prudhoe Bay. An Anchorage woman won $30,000 by coming within 60 seconds.

NOME

Gold Rus.

In terms of sheer pandemonium and skullduggery, the gold rush to Nome put Skagway and Dawson City in the shade.

By spring of 1899 about 5,000 prospectors and boomers had converged on the tent city on the shore of the Bering Sea. Many of them were busy jumping claims around Anvil Creek, in the hills a few miles inland, where 3 men known as "The Lucky Swedes" had made the original strike.

While the real miners fought among themselves, the remaining throngs of drifters and greenhorns milled about the beach. Thus, when someone discovered that the beach itself was laden with grains of gold, it was this army of n'er-do-wells who crowded shoulder-to-shoulder for miles along the shore to churn the sands and become wealthy.

They departed for Seattle in the fall, arriving with pokes of gold and vivid tales which spread quickly across the country. Meanwhile 1,500 fresh stampeders, having caught rumors drifting up the Yukon, boarded the last downriver stern wheeler from Dawson to Nome. They were followed down the river ice that winter by people with dog teams and horses, people walking, even an enterprising lad on a bicycle who prompted a surprised Indian to remark, "White man sit down, walk like crazy!"

Then the excitement began. In June, 1900 an armada of 230 ships began arriving at Nome to disgorge 20,000 people, who overnight transformed the 1-saloon town of 5,000 into a 100-saloon metropolis "2 blocks wide and 5 miles long."

While claim jumping and fraud proceeded apace among the miners

E.A. Hegg Collection University of Washington Libraries

off in the hills, and an epidemic of thievery, robbery and violence engulfed the town, the hordes along the beach were engrossed in their own particular madness.

The newcomers brought with them hundreds of indescribable machines hastily designed and fabricated for the purpose of separating gold from sand. Some were monsters on wheels, some involved treadmills, almost all were mistakes. During that summer, it is estimated, the thousands of beach boomers extracted a half million in gold with the aid of machines which had cost 3 or 4 times that amount.

By fall the bonanza on the beach was exhausted and 15 thousand people scrambled for ships bound for Seattle. The boom had lasted 3 months. But the miners back in the hills, once order had been restored among them, continued to develop the gold industry which would eventually sustain Nome through 60 years of ups and downs.

ome 1900 / looking South

Wm. & R. Hunt Collection/Alaska Historical Library

900

Fever

Nome Today

A huge granite rock sea wall, built in 1951 to deflect the howling Bering Sea storms which devastated Nome year after year, conceals the town beachfront which churned with humanity in 1899 and 1900. Farther along, however, an occasional hunk of rusted machinery juts from the sand as a monument to those frantic days. New and remodeled buildings dominate the few frame structures surviving from gold rush days. Although the price of gold has renewed some mining operations, Nome, with a population of about 3,500, including many Native people, now serves as a major service and supply center for the Seward Peninsula.

Nome 1900

Kotzebue

Kotzebue, just above the Arctic Circle and near the top of the Western Alaska area, is about the size of Barrow but has a higher proportion (80% of 3,000) of Eskimo people. It is probably the most typical modern Eskimo community easily accessible to visitors. But unlike the many small villages for which it serves as a commercial center, Kotzebue's 19th century log and hodge-podge frame dwellings are giving way to modern housing and commercial structures.

Its Native people still depend heavily on subsistence hunting and fishing, but the summer economy includes commercial fishing and tourism. Residents also herd reindeer— domesticated twins of the caribou— whose meat is marketed throughout Alaska while the antlers are ground into powder sold in Asia as an aphrodisiac. The nearby Kobuk Mts. yield jade chunks, the size of pianos, which are cut for sale to jewelry manufacturers.

On the outskirts of town is the "Kotzebue National Forest," a single scraggly black spruce brought from Southeast in 1958 and carefully nurtured since.

A Kotzebue woman tends a rack of fish meat hung to cure in the sun.

Leonhard Seppala, Nome, Alaska's greatest dog musher. Also shown with a few of his dogs (at right).

The Great Serum Run to Nome

When Nome was stricken by a diphtheria epidemic in 1925 there was a wireless transmitter to flash an urgent request for serum to be rushed up the Alaska Railroad to Nenana on the Tanana River. But the only feasible way to carry the serum across the miles of winter wilderness between Nenana and Nome was by dog sled.

In Nome Alaska's greatest dog musher, Leonhard Seppala, chose his 20 best dogs and set off across the treacherous ice cover on Norton Sound, headed for Nenana with his finest lead dog, Togo, at the fore. He left behind a freight dog named Balto.

Unknown to Seppala a new plan was being devised over the wireless. In winds at 60 below, Wild Bill Shannon departed Nenana as the first of a series of mushers who would relay the serum westward between villages and roadhouses scattered along the route.

About 250 miles out of Nome, after 4 days of fighting through minus-40 weather, Seppala met Henry Ivanoff, the 17th musher in the relay from Nenana. The exhausted Seppala re-

traced his trail for 91 miles before passing the serum to the waiting Charlie Olson, who carried it 25 miles to Gunnar Kaasen. Kaasen mushed the final 53 miles to Nome behind a borrowed lead dog: none other than the plodding Balto, plucked by Kaasen from Seppala's pack of rejects.

The long run by Seppala was by far the toughest, Kaasen's among the easier. But America's eye is on the finish line. Kaasen and Balto made headlines across the nation and were recruited to make a movie in California. Today children in New York City still gambol about a bronze likeness of Balto which was unveiled in Central Park. But 2 years after the famous run a visitor from Cleveland discovered Balto languishing as an exhibit in a Los Angeles carnival. The man's protests inspired a fund raising drive in Cleveland; the dog was purchased and installed as a prime attraction in the city's zoological gardens for many years.

As for Seppala's heroic but unsung Togo, he was sent to stud in a New England kennel where, like Balto, he lived to a ripe old age. History eventually acknowledged his feat to the extent that his remains were mounted by a taxidermist and displayed at Yale University until they were donated to a museum in Vermont. The effigy, later relegated to back-room storage, was recently discovered and acquired by an Anchorage taxidermist.

© Jim Lavrakas / Anchorage Daily News

*D*og sledding probably began among Eskimos in the 15th century, and it remained the primary mode of winter travel and transport in Alaska's vast bush country until pilots began pioneering air routes in the late 1920's. From 1908 to 1917 one of the highlights of Nome's year was the All-Alaska Sweepstakes, a 408-mile springtime race between Nome and the mining town of Candle, often won by the great musher Leonhard Seppala.

Dog Sleddin

*A*laskans take their sled dog racing as seriously as they do the Super Bowl and the World Series. No newspaper or newscast during the 1st half of March is complete without a progress report on the Iditarod Trail Sled Dog Race, in which upwards of 60 mushers drive more than 1,000 miles over hazardous terrain, in often bitter cold, between Anchorage and Nome. Their route follows an old mail and freight trail between Knik Arm and the mining town of Iditarod, then shoots north to meet the path followed by the mushers of the famous serum run to Nome.

In late February other long distance mushers depart from Fairbanks on the Yukon Quest Race over a 1,000-mile trail to Whitehorse, Yukon Territory.

An entirely different breed of mushers and dogs compete in numerous sprint

Alaska

Alaska (except warm Southeast) have attracted mushers from other states and 8 foreign countries. Some competitions are limited to juniors and women, but women are strong contenders in almost all races. Susan Butcher of

...aces, including the Anchorage Fur Rendezvous World Championship Race of three 25-mile heats; the North American Open Race of 3 heats totaling 70 miles, at Fairbanks; and the Alaska State Championships races in Soldotna, which award prizes in ... categories of team size.

More than two dozen sled dog races throughout

Manley twice placed 2nd in the grueling Iditarod; in 1985 a moose attacked her team, forcing her to withdraw. That race was taken by Libby Riddles, a young lady from Teller, near Nome, who jumped ahead by plunging into a dark storm over the open ice of Norton Sound while her rivals waited out the blow. Butcher came back to win the 1986 race in record breaking time.

Trained by the necessities of surviving in lean surroundings with a minimum of resources, the Eskimo became a superb craftsman. The **umiak** is one example, and Eskimo women are known as the only seamstresses in the world who can stitch waterproof seams.

The seamstresses followed two principal guidelines: they must make garments and footwear both waterproof and

Th

light. An Eskimo clad in **mukluks** (boots) and a 2-layer parka of caribou hide is warmer on an ice pack at 40 below than an urban American bundled in 5 times the weight of winter clothing.

Another Eskimo characteristic born of survival is adaptability, a trait which includes a strong talent for mastering the white man's mechanical products. An early explorer told of giving a pocket watch to an Eskimo who, when the watch finally

Northern Eskimo

failed, removed all its parts, oiled them, and restored the timepiece to perfect working order.

This innate ability has earned Eskimos a reputation as excellent mechanics and technicians. And their art of living together under harsh circumstances has also produced a number of highly skilled politicians.

Eskimos of Little Diomede Island using a New England style boat in 1917. White whalers often preferred the Eskimo umiaks.

Image vs. Fact

"Eskimos live in Igloos"

Igloos of ice and snow provided only temporary shelter and storage, Arctic Eskimos lived mostly in dwellings of sod laid upon frames of driftwood or whale bones. Western people also stretched animal hides over poles to make a teepee-like structure for warm weather use. Farther south the typical house was made of logs cut from inland river valleys.

"Eskimos are found only in the Far North"

Ancestors of the Eskimo came from Asia to migrate across the top of Alaska and along the west and south coasts. Eventually they occupied the entire coastline from the Arctic Ocean to the Alaska Peninsula, Kodiak Island and Prince William Sound.

"Eskimos subsist on whale meat"

Whale was a vital part of the coastal fare but Eskimos, depending upon their home area, had a surprisingly varied diet which might include some combination of sea mammals, fish, birds, eggs, roots, greens and such game as caribou, moose, Polar and Grizzly bears, and numerous smaller animals.

"Eskimos are 'born to stand the cold' "

Eskimos have no natural immunity to cold. They simply learned to dress sensibly, and found ingenious ways to do so. (Nor are they immune to fashion: modern Eskimos wear garments of nylon, fleece and down; the women make brightly colored ankle-length garments of cotton cloth, and similar shorter covers, called kuspuks, to cover conventional parkas.)

The Anchorage Museum

Southwest Alaska
& the Aleutian

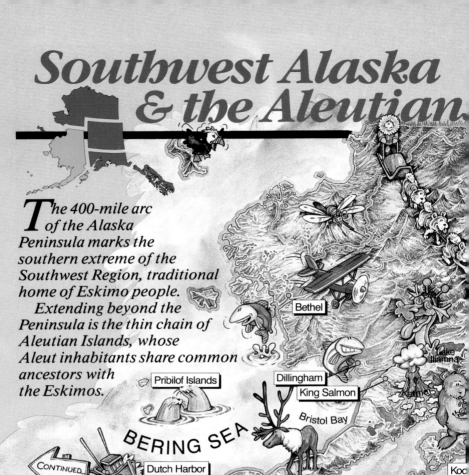

*T*he 400-mile arc
of the Alaska
Peninsula marks the
southern extreme of the
Southwest Region, traditional
home of Eskimo people.
  Extending beyond the
Peninsula is the thin chain of
Aleutian Islands, whose
Aleut inhabitants share common
ancestors with
the Eskimos.

Bethel

Pribilof Islands

Dillingham

King Salmon

Bristol Bay

Lake Iliamna

BERING SEA

CONTINUED.

Dutch Harbor

Koo

The Aleutians

The treeless Aleutian Islands, so windswept that the unremitting rains fall almost horizontally, are a chain of volcanic mountain tops stretching across the North Pacific to separate the cold Bering Sea from the warm Japanese current. The Aleuts, distant cousins of the Eskimos, were originally scattered throughout the islands in villages of sod dwellings. With unsurpassed seamanship they fished and hunted sea mammals, including whales, in Eskimo-style umiaks. Disease and a century of brutal Russian domination reduced a population exceeding 15,000 to about 900 in 1848. Today about 2,000 Aleuts occupy 11 communities on 7 islands.

World War in the

I n June of 1942, just 6 months after Pearl Harbor, Americans were stunned to learn that the Japanese had actually seized pieces of U.S. territory: the forlorn island of Attu, at the end of the Aleutian chain 1,200 miles from the mainland Alaska Peninsula, along with the neighboring island of Kiska.

But the nation's attention soon shifted to events in the distant South Pacific, while the campaign to recover the Aleutians proceeded amidst weather so foul that American planes bombed the Pribilof Islands in the belief that they were striking a

prove to be, more casualties were inflicted by frostbite and hypothermia than by the tough Japanese defenders.

Storming the beaches of Attu's Massacre Bay in May of 1943, American soldiers encountered for the first time the fanatical "banzai" spirit which would characterize Japanese troops throughout the war. The Attu battle ended with 2,351 Japanese killed or dead by suicide; only 28 were captured.

Over 34,000 U.S.

KISKA

ATTU

AMCHITKA

ADA

Japanese fleet.

Preparing to invade Attu, military commanders sought to deceive potential spies by equipping, clothing and briefing the troops for an African landing. As bloody as the Attu fight would

The Anchorage Museum

troops were then assembled to retake Kiska, but the atrocious Aleutian weather proved a blessing in disguise for both sides. The Japanese, under an impenetrable cover of fog, evacuated 5,000 men in less than a day. American invaders, fresh from the horrors of Attu, swarmed ashore to be met by a lonely mongrel dog named "Explosion," ecstatically waving his tail on the deserted shore. The dog, given months before by an American soldier to a civilian weather

Aleutians

observer on Kiska, had been captured along with his new owner. He now produced one of the rare high spots of the Aleutian campaign by swiftly locating his original master among the thousands of troops struggling shoreward through the wild surf.

The islands are still dotted with sagging quonset huts, deserted bunkers and the remains of downed aircraft, souvenirs of "The Forgotten War" that may have altered the entire course of the long struggle in the Pacific.

COLD BAY

DUTCH HARBOR

UMNAK

ATKA

The obscure conflict in the North Pacific was over. But had the Japanese thrown their Aleutian fleet into the Battle of Midway instead, they might well have won that crucial engagement in which the American navy halted the tide of Japanese advances across the Pacific. In the final analysis the American military profited greatly from numerous invaluable lessons learned in the Aleutians.

Kodiak just prior to World War II, nearing the end of a tranquil era.

Kodiak

The island city of Kodiak, known to gourmets around the world for its delicious king crab, began as the first permanent headquarters for the Russian reign over Alaska. One of the largest commercial fishing ports in the U.S., it is also a transfer point for ship cargo bound for the Aleutian Islands. The Kodiak island group is home to brown (grizzly) bears weighing up to 1,500 lbs., the largest carnivorous animals on the continent.

© 1985 Alissa Crandall / Alaska Photo

From his settlement at St. Paul (Kodiak) Alexander Baranof, manager of the Russian-American Co. and virtual ruler of Alaska, would set out with 1,000 Aleuts in 2-man *bidarkas*—a Russian adaptation of the *umiak*—in search of highly prized sea otter pelts. They crossed the treacherous Gulf of Alaska and plied the coast for 1,500 miles, paddling all the way to the Southeast panhandle. A warehouse for the sea otter pelts, built in the 1790's and known now as the Baranof Museum, stands not far from the Kodiak docks.

Kodiak's Russian Past

Venturing from the Kodiak base, Baranof's people erected a fort at Kenai and a shipyard near Seward, founded an agricultural colony at Yakutat Bay, and in 1799 built the post at Sitka to which he transferred his headquarters in 1802.

The 20 onion-domed churches which still dot Alaska's coastline, including the oldest at Kodiak, are a legacy of the 10 missionary monks who joined the colony in 1794 to establish the first Russian Orthodox parish in America. One of them, Father Herman, known for his compassion toward the Natives suffering so greatly under Russian domination, was canonized as a saint in 1970.

E.A. Hegg Collection/Alaska Historical Library

Wild Things

Among the forests, waters and mountain terrains surrounding the desolated valley live myriad wild animals, unhunted by men and subject only to the laws of survival. Dominated by the lordly brown bear and the hulking moose, the host of creatures includes the caribou, wolf, fox, wolverine, lynx, otter, beaver, porcupine, hare, marten, weasel, squirrel and vole.

Katmai
National Monument & Preserve

At the base of the Alaska Peninsula about 100 miles northwest of Kodiak lies Katmai National Monument and Preserve, centered around "The Valley of 10,000 Smokes," a stark moonscape created by one of the greatest volcano eruptions in history.

Most of the preserve's 4 million acres, however, is a breath-taking wilderness of glaciers, lakes, rivers, fjords, bays and lush green forest which, like Denali National Park, contains one of the most diverse concentrations of wildlife in Alaska.

And the fish, over 2 dozen species, draw sportsmen from throughout the world to Katmai and the surrounding area: Rainbow Trout, Dolly Varden, Lake Trout, Grayling and the Sockeye (Red) Salmon which ascend to the lakes a million strong and crowd the rivers so thickly that visitors are tempted to try walking on their backs.

Are Alaskan Fish Really That Big?

The hefty Rainbow Trout of the Katmai area, weighing up to 20 lbs., symbolize a problem which plagues Alaskan fishing people: the true statistics leave little room for creative exaggeration. Alaskans therefore tend to by-pass this obstacle with dazzling tales of matching wits with their finned adversaries, attributing to the fish intellectual powers not fully verified. Assertions concerning pounds, inches and feet, however, may be digested in their entirety.

The Valley of 10,000

O n June 6th, 1912, Mt. Novarupta, thought to be an extinct volcano, erupted with a fury that hurled 7 cubic miles of ash 50,000 ft. into the stratosphere. A white-hot blast of wind peeled forests from mountain sides or incinerated the trees to leave acres of carbonized stumps stabbing the air like burned-out match sticks.

In the depths of the earth forces beyond imagination sucked the insides out of Mt. Katmai, 7 miles away. Its top collapsed into a crater 3 miles across and 3,700 ft. deep from rim to bottom. More than 40 square miles of valley was buried under a mass of pumice and ash up to 700 ft. thick. All that remained of Mt. Novarupta was a mound of black rock, 800 ft. in diameter, protruding above the surface.

A southwest wind carried air-borne ash over most of Alaska, blanketing a 3,000-square-mile area under a choking cover of fine powder as much as a foot deep. Rocks rained into the sea 5 miles off shore. Kodiak was evacuated. The long summer days darkened into a night that lasted 60 days.

From streams and springs buried

© 1985 Harald Sund

The "smokes" have since expired, but the great valley remains so desolate and haunting to the eye that it was visited by astronauts as a means of preparing themselves for the experience of walking on the moon.

'mokes

under the smoldering debris, steam forced its way upward through cracks and vents. Four years later an expedition of scientists was awed by the spectacle of the huge valley filled, as far as the eye could see, with thousands of pillars of vapor rising 1,000 ft. into the air. They named it "The Valley of 10,000 Smokes," evoking an image which prompted the government in 1918 to establish Katmai National Monument.

Did You Know?

*N*ovarupta exploded with a force 9 times as powerful as the recent eruption of Mt. St. Helens in Washington State.

The sound was heard at least 700 miles away.

Ash from Novarupta traveled around the world. It is estimated that the gray pall decreased by 20% the amount of heat reaching earth from the sun at high noon.

Ice Fishing

strike, they may be on the verge of a veritable feeding frenzy which will incite them to gobble even unbaited hooks. It is the mystery of the black water, and the righteous rewards of patience, which prompt some Alaskans to break the monotony of long winters by wrapping themselves in mountains of cold weather duds and taking to the uncluttered frozen lakes.

Purists may fish only by night, chop ice holes with hatchets, and sit on upturned buckets. More social types will drive campers onto the ice by daylight, employ gasoline powered ice augers, and bring ham and eggs with them just in case. Either way, ice fishing separates the contemplative from the restless. Elbow-to-elbow fishing is seldom a problem unless—and Alaskans are funny that way—you bring your own crowd with you.

The winter night is black as pitch. On the frozen surface of a lake two figures huddle in the light of a lantern which sheds a pool of pale light on the hole in the ice at their feet and on the tiny skid shack behind them. They stare fixedly at the hairline ripples where two fishing lines, draped lightly over their mittens, disappear into the darkness of the exposed water.

A few feet beneath their stools an enormous school of fish may be brushing against baited hooks. Or there may be nothing but empty water. But if and when the fish

ing mission in Alaska, are said to have spotted huge, dark shapes lurking below the surface. A local resident once thought he spied a boat moving through the choppy water, but closer inspection revealed what he described as a dorsal fin.

Elsewhere in the world fresh water sturgeon have been known to reach 20-ft. length and weigh a ton, and medium-size sturgeon have been taken from Iliamna. The lake also contains giant squid and a species of fresh water seals, and beluga whales are seen chasing salmon upriver to the Iliamna outlet. One of those, perhaps, might explain the disappearance of a 55-gallon oil drum from which an Iliamna man had suspended a hook

The notorious Aleutian Island winds howl up the Alaska Peninsula to race the 80-mile length of Lake Iliamna, churning its dark waters into whitecaps. It is the largest fresh water lake entirely within

Legends of the

U.S. borders, and 1,000 feet deep: enough to conceal the creature which, according to Indian legends of old, would cause anyone who viewed it to shrivel and die.

In modern times, it's reported, a bush pilot dropped a baited halibut hook on aircraft cable tied to a strut on his float plane. Something took the bait and tore off the strut. Two astronauts, flying a plane over Iliamna during a train-

baited with a hindquarters of moose.

Whatever the case, it is a rare visitor indeed who can scan the somber, cold waters of Lake Iliamna with a completely disbelieving eye.

King (Chinook) Salmon

Rainbow Trout

Pink Salmon

Alaskan Fishing

© 1985 Rick Furniss / Alaska Photo

With good reason sports fishing buffs from far-flung parts of the world travel to Alaska in search of the ultimate fishing experience. The 20-lb. Rainbow Trout of the Katmai region or the 495-lb. Pacific Halibut taken near Petersburg are not run-of-the-water specimens, but the size, variety and numbers of fish in Alaska are extraordinary. Good fishing spots near urban areas, especially Anchorage, tend to be crowded with anglers in summertime, but the common use of the bush plane gives ready access to remote and bountiful fishing spots among the state's uncounted rivers, lakes and bays.

Did You Know?

The small Blackfish, found only in Alaska and eastern Siberia, is one of only two species (the other is the tropical swamp eel) which have evolved an esophagus enabling them to breathe oxygen from the atmosphere.

Red Salmon

Arctic Grayling

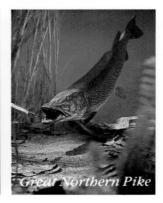

Great Northern Pike

Marine
Life

The frigid waters of the Bering Sea, extending northward from the Aleutian Islands and separating Alaska from Siberia, are enlivened by a host of creatures from whales to fur seal and salmon. Among the most intriguing are the hulking walrus, some weighing more than a ton and a half. About 200,000 of the tusked monsters (80% of the world population) inhabit Alaskan waters, notably the Bering Sea. They spend most of their lives drifting about on the ice, diving to the sea bottom to feed on mollusk, mating and giving birth between

© 1985 Steve McCutcheon

Stellar Sea Lions bask in the soggy air of an Aleutian island.

of the Aleutians
& the Bering Sea

December and April. But as the ice recedes to the north in summer, the bulls leave cows and offspring to fend for themselves and swim south for an all male get-together in Bristol Bay. There they congregate at a few isolated retreats such as tiny Round Island, where naturalists also gather from around the globe to witness 7 to 8 thousand of the giants engaged in their annual shoulder-to-shoulder "bull session."

135

In chill isolation on the Bering Sea, 240 miles remote from even the remote Aleutians, lie the barren Pribilof Islands, to which 80% of the world's fur seal population migrates each year to give birth and mate. So frequently is the area engulfed in fog that after a Russian explorer happened upon St. George Island in 1786,

The Pribilof Islands

a year passed before St. Paul was discovered just 40 miles away.

Having been slaughtered to near-extinction—first by Russian fur traders on the Pribilofs and later by the ships of several nations which intercepted the migrating seals at sea—the herd now numbers about 1½ million after 75 years of harvesting controlled by the U.S. government.

The beaches and shoreline waters turn dark with seals each summer, the air resounding with roars and moans as large bulls called "beachmasters" round up their harems of up to 100 females and savagely repel any other male which attempts to intrude.

Two small and uninhabited islands, Walrus and Otter, became literally blanketed by sea birds, over 190 species in all, which migrate to the Pribilofs at the same time of year. However St. George provides the nesting ground for 90% of the birds, while 80% of the Pribilof seal population converges on St. Paul.

© 1985 Steve McCutcheon

© 1985 Art Wolfe / Alaska Photo

Seals of the Pribilofs

The islands of St. George and St. Paul palpitate with life and reverberate with noise as hundreds of thousands of birds swoop and swirl over the dark masses of seals along the shore.

For 2 months the bull seals are too busy—organizing their harems, fighting and mating—to eat. The females cannot be diverted from choosing their own sites, but that qualification aside, the bulls are fierce about ruling their individual territories. They use their teeth to seize any straying female and toss her back into place.

About 350,000 pups are born each summer on the Pribilofs. Females are pregnant almost constantly, for nature has equipped them with a 2nd uterus which is impregnated within hours of the birth of a lone cub.

The bulls, first to arrive in spring, are first to depart, in August. About 2 months later the females will go too, leaving the pups to fend for themselves on the beach. Eventually they, too respond to that instinct which calls them into the sea, where they may swim for 2 years before sighting the Pribilofs again.

Birds, Birds

Horned Puffins

Kittiwake

Birds

Red Faced Cormorant

I f Alaska's scenery commands the eye, and its wildlife captures the imagination, there is also drama in its skies. Eagles, relatively plentiful here as compared to their small numbers elsewhere, perhaps come first to mind as symbolic of Alaska. But to Alaskans the Raven may be viewed as the most Alaskan bird of all. The cultures of most Alaska Native groups are rich with traditions which associate the great black birds with stories of the Creation. In any event, the two share their domain with a colorful crowd. Over 350 species of birds have been spotted in Alaska, about 150 of which reside year-round. Migrating birds arrive from distant points in Asia, Hawaii and South America, some flying as much as 25,000 miles round trip.

Arctic Tern

Auklet

We Hope You've made some good friends in Alaska

*W*e've left things unsaid, of course. But we trust you'll meet some of the many Alaskans who leave absolutely nothing unsaid to an ear that's willing to listen. They bear listening to, because whatever outlandish thing they may tell you, chances are it'll eventually turn out to be true ... more or less.

Please Visit Us Again

Index

For further reading:
*Your library or book store has
many books about Alaska. A few
are listed here:*

"ALASKA GEOGRAPHIC"
  series *of books, The Alaska
  Geographic Society*
ALASKA, High Roads to
  Adventure, *National
  Geographic Society*
THE RACE TO NOME,
  Kenneth A. Ungermann
MONUMENTS IN CEDAR,
  Edward L. Keithahn
MT. McKINLEY THE PIONEER
  CLIMBS, *Terris Moore*
ONE MAN'S GOLD RUSH,
  Murray Morgan
THE KLONDIKE FEVER,
  Pierre Berton
ANCHORAGE, STAR OF THE
  NORTH, *Evangeline Atwood*
E.T. BARNETTE, *Terrence Cole*
LORD OF ALASKA, *Baranov
  and the Russian Adventure,
  Hector Chevigny*
A JOURNEY THROUGH
  PRINCE WILLIAM
  SOUND, *Alaska Heritage
  Enterprises Inc.*